3D Deep Learning with Python

Design and develop your computer vision model with 3D data
using PyTorch3D and more

Xudong Ma

Vishakh Hegde

Lilit Yolyan

BIRMINGHAM—MUMBAI

3D Deep Learning with Python

Publishing Product Manager: Dinesh Chaudhary
Content Development Editor: Joseph Sunil
Technical Editor: Rahul Limbachiya
Copy Editor: Safis Editing
Project Coordinator: Farheen Fathima
Proofreader: Safis Editing
Indexer: Rekha Nair
Production Designer: Ponraj Dhandapani
Marketing Coordinator: Shifa Ansari

First published: November 2022

Production reference: 1211022

Published by Packt Publishing Ltd.
Livery Place
35 Livery Street
Birmingham
B3 2PB, UK.

ISBN 978-1-80324-782-3

www.packt.com

"To my wife and family, for their support and encouragement at every step". - Vishakh Hegde

"To my family and friends, whose love and support have been my biggest motivation". - Lilit Yolyan

Contributors

About the author

Xudong Ma is a Staff Machine Learning engineer with Grabango Inc. in Berkeley California. He was a Senior Machine Learning Engineer at Facebook (Meta) Oculus and worked closely with the 3D PyTorch Team on 3D facial tracking projects. He has many years of experience working on computer vision, machine learning, and deep learning and holds a Ph.D. in Electrical and Computer Engineering.

Vishakh Hegde is a Machine Learning and Computer Vision researcher. He has over 7 years of experience in the field, during which he has authored multiple well-cited research papers and published patents. He holds a masters from Stanford University specializing in applied mathematics and machine learning, and a BS and MS in Physics from IIT Madras. He previously worked at Schlumberger and Matroid. He is a Senior Applied Scientist at Ambient.ai, where he helped build their weapon detection system which is deployed at several Global Fortune 500 companies. He is now leveraging his expertise and passion for solving business challenges to build a technology startup in Silicon Valley. You can learn more about him on his website.

I would like to thank the computer vision researchers whose breakthrough research I got to write about. I want to thank the reviewers for their feedback and the wonderful team at Packt Publishing for giving me the chance to be creative. Finally, I want to thank my wife and family for all their support and encouragement when I most needed it.

Lilit Yolyan is a machine learning researcher working on her Ph.D. at YSU. Her research focuses on building computer vision solutions for smart cities using remote sensing data. She has 5 years of experience in the field of computer vision and has worked on a complex driver safety solution to be deployed by many well-known car manufacturing companies.

About the reviewer

Eya Abid is a Masters of Engineering student specializing in Deep Learning and Computer Vision. She holds the position of an AI instructor within NVIDIA and quantum machine learning at CERN.

I would like to dedicate this work first to my family, friends, and whoever helped me through this process. A special dedication to Aymen, to whom I am forever grateful.

Ramesh Sekhar is the CEO and co-founder of Dapster.ai, a company that builds affordable and easily deployable robots that perform the most arduous tasks in warehouses. Ramesh has worked at companies like Symbol, Motorola, and Zebra and specializes in building products at the intersection of computer vision, AI, and Robotics. He has a BS in Electrical Engineering and an MS in Computer Science. Ramesh founded Dapster.ai in 2020. Dapster's mission is to build robots that positively impact human beings by performing dangerous and unhealthy tasks. Their vision is to unlock better jobs, fortify supply chains, and better negotiate the challenges arising from climate change.

Utkarsh Srivastava is an AI/ML professional, trainer, YouTuber, and blogger. He loves to tackle and develop ML, NLP, and computer vision algorithms to solve complex problems. He started his data science career as a blogger on his blog (datamahadev.com) and YouTube channel (datamahadev), followed by working as a senior data science trainer at an institute in Gujarat. Additionally, he has trained and counseled 1,000+ working professionals and students in AI/ML. Utkarsh has completed 40+ freelance training and development work/projects in data science and analytics, AI/ML, Python development, and SQL. He hails from Lucknow and is currently settled in Bangalore, India, as an analyst at Deloitte USI Consulting.

I would like to thank my mother, Mrs. Rupam Srivastava, for her continuous guidance and support throughout my hardships and struggles. Thanks also to the Supreme Para-Brahman.

Mason McGough is a Sr. R&D Engineer and Computer Vision Specialist at Lowe's Innovation Labs. He has a passion for imaging and has spent over a decade solving computer vision problems across a broad range of industrial and academic disciplines including geology, bio-informatics, game development, and retail. Most recently he is exploring the use of Digital Twins and 3D scanning for retail stores.

I wish to thank Andy Lykos, Joseph Canzano, Alexander Arango, Oleg Alexander, Erin Clark, and my family for their support.

Table of Contents

PART 1: 3D Data Processing Basics

1

2

PART 2: 3D Deep Learning Using PyTorch3D

3

4

5

PART 3: State-of-the-art 3D Deep Learning Using PyTorch3D

7

8

9

Performing End-to-End View Synthesis with SynSin   169

10

Mesh R-CNN   189

Index   209

Other Books You May Enjoy   216

Preface

Developers working with 3D computer vision will be able to put their knowledge to work with this practical guide to 3D deep learning. The book provides a hands-on approach to implementation and associated methodologies that will have you up and running and productive in no time.

Complete with step-by-step explanations of essential concepts, practical examples, and self-assessment questions, you will begin by exploring state-of-the-art 3D deep learning.

You will learn about basic 3D mesh and point cloud data processing using PyTorch3D, such as loading and saving PLY and OBJfiles, projecting 3D points onto camera coordinates using perspective camera models or orthographic camera models, and rendering point clouds and meshes to images, among other things. You will also learn how to implement certain state-of-the-art 3D deep learning algorithms, such as differential rendering, NeRF, SynSin, and Mesh R-CNN because coding for these deep learning models becomes easier using the PyTorch3D library.

By the end of this book, you will be able to implement your own 3D deep learning models.

Who this book is for

This book is for beginners and intermediate-level machine learning practitioners, data scientists, machine learning engineers, and deep learning engineers who are looking to become well-versed in computer vision techniques using 3D data.

What this book covers

Chapter 1, Introducing 3D Data Processing, will cover the basics of 3D data, such as how 3D data is stored and the basic concepts of meshes and point clouds, world coordinations, and camera coordinations. It also shows us what NDC is (a frequently used coordination), how to convert between different coordinations, perspective cameras, and orthographic cameras, and which camera models should be used.

Chapter 2, Introducing 3D Computer Vision and Geometry, will show us the basic concepts in computer graphics, such as rendering and shading. We will learn about some fundamental concepts that will be required in the later chapters of this book, including, 3D geometry transforms, PyTorch tensors, and optimization.

Chapter 3, Fitting Deformable Mesh Models to Raw Point Clouds, will present a hands-on project of using a deformable 3D model to fit a noisy 3D observation using all the knowledge that we have learned in the previous chapters. We will explore frequently used cost functions, why these cost functions are important, and when these cost functions are usually used. Finally, we will explore a concrete example of which cost functions have been selected for which tasks and how to set up the optimization loop to obtain the results that we want.

Chapter 4, *Learning Object Pose Detection and Tracking by Differentiable Rendering*, will talk about the basic concepts of differentiable rendering. It will help you understand the basic concepts and know when you can apply these techniques to solve your own problems.

Chapter 5, *Understanding Differentiable Volumetric Rendering*, will present a hands-on project using differentiable rendering to estimate camera positions from a single image and a known 3D mesh model. We will learn how to practically use PyTorch3D to set up cameras, renders, and shaders. We will also get hands-on experience in using different cost functions to get optimization results.

Chapter 6, *Exploring Neural Radiance Fields (NeRF)*, will provide a hands-on project using differentiable rendering to estimate 3D mesh models from several images and texture models.

Chapter 7, *Exploring Controllable Neural Feature Fields*, will cover a very important algorithm for view synthesis, which is NeRF. We will learn what it is all about, how to use it, and where it is valuable.

Chapter 8, *Modeling the Human Body in 3D*, will explore 3D human body fitting using the SMPL algorithm.

Chapter 9, *Performing End-to-End View Synthesis with SynSin*, will cover SynSin, which is a state-of-the-art deep learning image synthesis model.

Chapter 10, *Mesh R-CNN*, will introduce us to Mesh R-CNN, which is another state-of-the-art method for predicting 3D voxel models from a single input image.

To get the most out of this book

Software/hardware covered in the book	Operating system requirements
Python 3.6+	Windows, macOS, or Linux

If you are using the digital version of this book, we advise you to type the code yourself or access the code from the book's GitHub repository (a link is available in the next section). Doing so will help you avoid any potential errors related to copying and pasting code.

Please check out these papers for reference:

Chapter 6: https://arxiv.org/abs/2003.08934, https://github.com/yenchenlin/nerf-pytorch

Chapter 7: https://m-niemeyer.github.io/project-pages/giraffe/index.html, https://arxiv.org/abs/2011.12100

Chapter 8: https://smpl.is.tue.mpg.de/, https://smplify.is.tue.mpg.de/, https://smpl-x.is.tue.mpg.de/

Chapter 9: https://arxiv.org/pdf/1912.08804.pdf

Chapter 10: https://arxiv.org/abs/1703.06870, https://arxiv.org/abs/1906.02739

Download the example code files

You can download the example code files for this book from GitHub at https://github.com/PacktPublishing/3D-Deep-Learning-with-Python. If there's an update to the code, it will be updated in the GitHub repository.

We also have other code bundles from our rich catalog of books and videos available at https://github.com/PacktPublishing/. Check them out!

Download the color images

We also provide a PDF file that has color images of the screenshots and diagrams used in this book. You can download it here: https://packt.link/WJr0Q.

Conventions used

There are a number of text conventions used throughout this book.

`Code in text`: Indicates code words in text, database table names, folder names, filenames, file extensions, pathnames, dummy URLs, user input, and Twitter handles. Here is an example: " Next, we need to update the `./options/options.py` file"

A block of code is set as follows:

```
elif opt.dataset == 'kitti':
    opt.min_z = 1.0
    opt.max_z = 50.0
    opt.train_data_path = (
        './DATA/dataset_kitti/'
    )
    from data.kitti import KITTIDataLoader
    return KITTIDataLoader
```

When we wish to draw your attention to a particular part of a code block, the relevant lines or items are set in bold:

```
wget https://dl.fbaipublicfiles.com/synsin/checkpoints/
realestate/synsin.pth
```

Any command-line input or output is written as follows:

```
bash ./download_models.sh
```

Bold: Indicates a new term, an important word, or words that you see onscreen. For instance, words in menus or dialog boxes appear in **bold**. Here is an example: "The refinement module (**g**) gets inputs from the neural point cloud renderer and then outputs the final reconstructed image."

> **Tips or important notes**
> Appear like this.

Get in touch

Feedback from our readers is always welcome.

General feedback: If you have questions about any aspect of this book, email us at customercare@packtpub.com and mention the book title in the subject of your message.

Errata: Although we have taken every care to ensure the accuracy of our content, mistakes do happen. If you have found a mistake in this book, we would be grateful if you would report this to us. Please visit www.packtpub.com/support/errata and fill in the form.

Piracy: If you come across any illegal copies of our works in any form on the internet, we would be grateful if you would provide us with the location address or website name. Please contact us at copyright@packt.com with a link to the material.

If you are interested in becoming an author: If there is a topic that you have expertise in and you are interested in either writing or contributing to a book, please visit authors.packtpub.com.

Share Your Thoughts

Once you've read *3D Deep Learning with Python*, we'd love to hear your thoughts! Scan the QR code below to go straight to the Amazon review page for this book and share your feedback.

https://packt.link/r/1-803-24782-7

Your review is important to us and the tech community and will help us make sure we're delivering excellent quality content.

Download a free PDF copy of this book

Thanks for purchasing this book!

Do you like to read on the go but are unable to carry your print books everywhere?

Is your eBook purchase not compatible with the device of your choice?

Don't worry, now with every Packt book you get a DRM-free PDF version of that book at no cost.

Read anywhere, any place, on any device. Search, copy, and paste code from your favorite technical books directly into your application.

The perks don't stop there, you can get exclusive access to discounts, newsletters, and great free content in your inbox daily

Follow these simple steps to get the benefits:

1. Scan the QR code or visit the link below

https://packt.link/free-ebook/9781803247823

2. Submit your proof of purchase
3. That's it! We'll send your free PDF and other benefits to your email directly

PART 1: 3D Data Processing Basics

This first part of the book will define the most basic concepts for data and image processing since these concepts are essential to our later discussions. This part of the book makes the book self-contained so that readers do not need to read any other books to get started with learning about PyTorch3D.

This part includes the following chapters:

- *Chapter 1, Introducing 3D Data Processing*
- *Chapter 2, Introducing 3D Computer Vision and Geometry*

1

Introducing 3D Data Processing

In this chapter, we are going to discuss some basic concepts that are very fundamental to 3D deep learning and that will be used frequently in later chapters. We will begin by learning about the most frequently used 3D data formats, as well as the many ways that we are going to manipulate them and convert them to different formats. We will start by setting up our development environment and installing all the necessary software packages, including Anaconda, Python, PyTorch, and PyTorch3D. We will then talk about the most frequently used ways to represent 3D data – for example, point clouds, meshes, and voxels. We will then move on to the 3D data file formats, such as PLY and OBJ files. We will then discuss 3D coordination systems. Finally, we will discuss camera models, which are mostly related to how 3D data is mapped to 2D images.

After reading this chapter, you will be able to debug 3D deep learning algorithms easily by inspecting output data files. With a solid understanding of coordination systems and camera models, you will be ready to build on that knowledge and learn about more advanced 3D deep learning topics.

In this chapter, we're going to cover the following main topics:

- Setting up a development environment and installing Anaconda, PyTorch, and PyTorch3D
- 3D data representation
- 3D data formats – PLY and OBJ files
- 3D coordination systems and conversion between them
- Camera models – perspective and orthographic cameras

Technical requirements

In order to run the example code snippets in this book, you will need to have a computer ideally with a GPU. However, running the code snippets with only CPUs is possible.

The recommended computer configuration includes the following:

- A GPU such as the GTX series or RTX series with at least 8 GB of memory
- Python 3
- The PyTorch library and PyTorch3D libraries

The code snippets for this chapter can be found at `https://github.com/PacktPublishing/3D-Deep-Learning-with-Python`.

Setting up a development environment

Let us first set up a development environment for all the coding exercises in this book. We recommend using a Linux machine for all the Python code examples in this book:

1. We will first set up Anaconda. Anaconda is a widely used Python distribution that bundles with the powerful CPython implementation. One advantage of using Anaconda is its package management system, enabling users to create virtual environments easily. The individual edition of Anaconda is free for solo practitioners, students, and researchers. To install Anaconda, we recommend visiting the website, `anaconda.com`, for detailed instructions. The easiest way to install Anaconda is usually by running a script downloaded from their website. After setting up Anaconda, run the following command to create a virtual environment of Python 3.7:

    ```
    $ conda create -n python3d python=3.7
    ```

    This command will create a virtual environment with Python version 3.7. In order to use this virtual environment, we need to activate it first by running the command:

2. Activate the newly created virtual environments with the following command:

    ```
    $ source activate python3d
    ```

3. Install PyTorch. Detailed instructions on installing PyTorch can be found on its web page at `www.pytorch.org/get-started/locally/`. For example, I will install PyTorch 1.9.1 on my Ubuntu desktop with CUDA 11.1, as follows:

    ```
    $ conda install pytorch torchvision torchaudio
    cudatoolkit-11.1 -c pytorch -c nvidia
    ```

4. Install PyTorch3D. PyTorch3D is an open source Python library for 3D computer vision recently released by Facebook AI Research. PyTorch3D provides many utility functions to easily manipulate 3D data. Designed with deep learning in mind, almost all 3D data can be handled by mini-batches, such as cameras, point clouds, and meshes. Another key feature of PyTorch3D is the implementation of a very important 3D deep learning technique, called *differentiable rendering*. However, the biggest advantage of PyTorch3D as a 3D deep learning library is its close ties to PyTorch.

PyTorch3D may need some dependencies, and detailed instructions on how to install these dependencies can be found on the PyTorch3D GitHub home page at `github.com/facebookresearch/pytorch3d`. After all the dependencies have been installed by following the instructions from the website, installing PyTorch3D can be easily done by running the following command:

```
$ conda install pytorch3d -c pytorch3d
```

Now that we have set up the development environment, let's go ahead and start learning data representation.

3D data representation

In this section, we will learn the most frequently used data representation of 3D data. Choosing data representation is a particularly important design decision for many 3D deep learning systems. For example, point clouds do not have grid-like structures, thus convolutions cannot be usually used directly for them. Voxel representations have grid-like structures; however, they tend to consume a high amount of computer memory. We will discuss the pros and cons of these 3D representations in more detail in this section. Widely used 3D data representations usually include point clouds, meshes, and voxels.

Understanding point cloud representation

A 3D point cloud is a very straightforward representation of 3D objects, where each point cloud is just a collection of 3D points, and each 3D point is represented by one three-dimensional tuple (x, y, or z). The raw measurements of many depth cameras are usually 3D point clouds.

From a deep learning point of view, 3D point clouds are one of the unordered and irregular data types. Unlike regular images, where we can define neighboring pixels for each individual pixel, there are no clear and regular definitions for neighboring points for each point in a point cloud – that is, convolutions usually cannot be applied to point clouds. Thus, special types of deep learning models need to be used for processing point clouds, such as PointNet: `https://arxiv.org/abs/1612.00593`.

Another issue for point clouds as training data for 3D deep learning is the heterogeneous data issue – that is, for one training dataset, different point clouds may contain different numbers of 3D points. One approach for avoiding such a heterogeneous data issue is forcing all the point clouds to have the same number of points. However, this may not be always possible – for example, the number of points returned by depth cameras may be different from frame to frame.

The heterogeneous data may create some difficulties for mini-batch gradient descent in training deep learning models. Most deep learning frameworks assume that each mini-batch contains training examples of the same size and dimensions. Such homogeneous data is preferred because it can be most efficiently processed by modern parallel processing hardware, such as GPUs. Handling heterogeneous mini-batches in an efficient way needs some additional work. Luckily, PyTorch3D provides many ways of handling heterogeneous mini-batches efficiently, which are important for 3D deep learning.

Understanding mesh representation

Meshes are another widely used 3D data representation. Like points in point clouds, each mesh contains a set of 3D points called vertices. In addition, each mesh also contains a set of polygons called faces, which are defined on vertices.

In most data-driven applications, meshes are a result of post-processing from raw measurements of depth cameras. Often, they are manually created during the process of 3D asset design. Compared to point clouds, meshes contain additional geometric information, encode topology, and have surface-normal information. This additional information becomes especially useful in training learning models. For example, graph convolutional neural networks usually treat meshes as graphs and define convolutional operations using the vertex neighboring information.

Just like point clouds, meshes also have similar heterogeneous data issues. Again, PyTorch3D provides efficient ways for handling heterogeneous mini-batches for mesh data, which makes 3D deep learning efficient.

Understanding voxel representation

Another important 3D data representation is voxel representation. A voxel is the counterpart of a pixel in 3D computer vision. A pixel is defined by dividing a rectangle in 2D into smaller rectangles and each small rectangle is one pixel. Similarly, a voxel is defined by dividing a 3D cube into smaller-sized cubes and each cube is called one voxel. The processes are shown in the following figure:

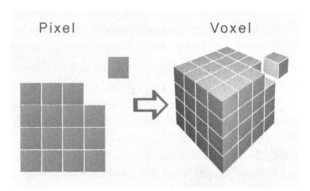

Figure 1.1 – Voxel representation is the 3D counterpart of 2D pixel representation, where a cubic space is divided into small volume elements

Voxel representations usually use **Truncated Signed Distance Functions** (**TSDFs**) to represent 3D surfaces. A **Signed Distance Function** (**SDF**) can be defined at each voxel as the (signed) distance between the center of the voxel to the closest point on the surface. A positive sign in an SDF indicates that the voxel center is outside an object. The only difference between a TSDF and an SDF is that the values of a TSDF are truncated, such that the values of a TSDF always range from -1 to +1.

Unlike point clouds and meshes, voxel representation is ordered and regular. This property is like pixels in images and enables the use of convolutional filters in deep learning models. One potential disadvantage of voxel representation is that it usually requires more computer memory, but this can be reduced by using techniques such as hashing. Nevertheless, voxel representation is an important 3D data representation.

There are 3D data representations other than the ones mentioned here. For example, multi-view representations use multiple images taken from different viewpoints to represent a 3D scene. RGB-D representations use an additional depth channel to represent a 3D scene. However, in this book, we will not be diving too deep into these 3D representations. Now that we have learned the basics of 3D data representations, we will dive into a few commonly used file formats for point clouds and meshes.

3D data file format – Ply files

The PLY file format was developed in the mid-1990s by a group of researchers from Stanford University. It has since evolved into one of the most widely used 3D data file formats. The file format has both an ASCII version and a binary version. The binary version is preferred in cases where file sizes and processing efficiencies are needed. The ASCII version makes it quite easy to debug. Here, we will discuss the basic format of PLY files and how to use both Open3D and PyTorch3D to load and visualize 3D data from PLY files.

In this section, we are going to discuss the two most frequently used data file formats to represent point clouds and meshes, the PLY file format and the OBJ file format. We are going to discuss the formats and how to load and save these file formats using PyTorch3D. PyTorch3D provides excellent utility functions, so loading from and saving to these file formats is efficient and easy using these utility functions.

An example, a cube.ply file, is shown in the following code snippet:

```
ply
format ascii 1.0
comment created for the book 3D Deep Learning with Python
element vertex 8
property float32 x
property float32 y
property float32 z
element face 12
property list uint8 int32 vertex_indices
end_header
-1 -1 -1
1 -1 -1
```

```
1  1  -1
-1  1  -1
-1  -1  1
1  -1  1
1  1  1
-1  1  1
3  0  1  2
3  5  4  7
3  6  2  1
3  3  7  4
3  7  3  2
3  5  1  0
3  0  2  3
3  5  7  6
3  6  1  5
3  3  4  0
3  7  2  6
3  5  0  4
```

As seen here, each PLY file contains a header part and a data part. The first line of every ASCII PLY file is always `ply`, which indicates that this is a PLY file. The second line, `format ascii 1.0`, shows that the file is of the Ascii type with a version number. Any lines starting with `comment` will be considered as a comment line, and thus anything following `comment` will be ignored when the PLY file is loaded by a computer. The `element vertex 8` line means that the first type of data in the PLY file is vertex and we have eight vertices. `property float32 x` means that each vertex has a property named x of the `float32 type`. Similarly, each vertex also has y and z properties. Here, each vertex is one 3D point. The `element face 12 line` means that the second type of data in this PLY file is of the `face` type and we have 12 faces. `property list unit8 int32 vertex_indices` shows that each face will be a list of vertex indices. The header part of the `ply` file always ends with an `end_header` line.

The first part of the data part of the PLY file consists of eight lines, where each line is the record for one vertex. The three numbers in each line represent the three x, y, and z properties of the vertex. For example, the three numbers -1, -1, -1 specify that the vertex has an x coordinate of -1, y coordinate of -1, and z coordinate of -1.

The second part of the data part of the ply file consists of 12 lines, where each line is the record for one face. The first number in the sequence of numbers indicates the number of vertices that the face has, and the following numbers are the vertex indices. The vertex indices are determined by the order that the vertices are declared in the PLY file.

We can use both Open3D and PyTorch3D to open the preceding file. Open3D is a Python package that is very handy for visualizing 3D data, and PyTorch3D is handy for using this data for deep learning models. The following is a code snippet, ply_example1.py, for visualizing the mesh in the cube. ply file and loading the vertices and meshes as PyTorch tensors:

```
import open3d
from pytorch3d.io import load_ply

mesh_file = "cube.ply"
print('visualizing the mesh using open3D')
mesh = open3d.io.read_triangle_mesh(mesh_file)
open3d.visualization.draw_geometries([mesh],
        mesh_show_wireframe = True,
        mesh_show_back_face = True)

print("Loading the same file with PyTorch3D")
vertices, faces = load_ply(mesh_file)
print('Type of vertices = ', type(vertices))
print("type of faces = ", type(faces))
print('vertices = ', vertices)
print('faces = ', faces)
```

In the preceding Python code snippet, a cube.ply mesh file is first opened by the open3d package by using the read_triangle_mesh function and all the 3D data is read into the mesh variable. The mesh can then be visualized using the Open3D library draw_geometries function. When you run this function, the Open3D library will pop up a window for interactively visualizing the mesh – that is, you can rotate, zoom into, and zoom out of the mesh using your mouse interactively. The cube.ply file, as you can guess, defines a mesh of a cube with eight vertices and six sides, where each side is covered by two faces.

We can also use the PyTorch3D library to load the same mesh. However, this time, we are going to obtain several PyTorch tensors – for example, one tensor for vertices and one tensor for faces. These tensors can be input into any PyTorch deep learning model directly. In this example, the load_ply function returns a tuple of vertices and faces, both of which are conventionally in the format of PyTorch tensors. When you run this ply_example1.py code snippet, the returned vertices should be a PyTorch tensor with a shape of [8, 3] – that is, there are eight vertices, and each vertex has three coordinates. Similarly, the returned faces should be a PyTorch tensor with a shape of [12, 3], that is, there are 12 faces, and each face has 3 vertex indices.

In the following code snippet, we show another example of the `parallel_plane_mono.ply` file, which can also be downloaded from our GitHub repository. The only difference between the mesh in this example and the mesh in the `cube is.ply` file is the number of faces. Instead of the six sides of a cube, here we have only four faces, which form two parallel planes:

```
ply
format ascii 1.0
comment created for the book 3D Deep Learning with Python
element vertex 8
property float32 x
property float32 y
property float32 z
element face 4
property list uint8 int32 vertex_indices
end_header
-1 -1 -1
1 -1 -1
1 1 -1
-1 1 -1
-1 -1 1
1 -1 1
1 1 1
-1 1 1
3 0 1 2
3 0 2 3
3 5 4 7
3 5 7 6
```

The mesh can be interactively visualized by the following `ply_example2.py`:

1. First, we import all the needed Python libraries:

    ```
    import open3d
    from pytorch3d.io import load_ply
    ```

2. We load the mesh using `open3d`:

```
mesh_file = "parallel_plane_mono.ply"
print('visualizing the mesh using open3D')
mesh = open3d.io.read_triangle_mesh(mesh_file)
```

3. We use `draw_geometries` to open a window for visualizing interactively with the mesh:

```
open3d.visualization.draw_geometries([mesh],
                    mesh_show_wireframe = True,
                    mesh_show_back_face = True)
```

4. We use `pytorch3d` to open the same mesh:

```
print("Loading the same file with PyTorch3D")
vertices, faces = load_ply(mesh_file)
```

5. We can print out the information about the loaded vertices and faces. In fact, they are just ordinary PyTorch3D tensors:

```
print('Type of vertices = ', type(vertices), ", type of
faces = ", type(faces))
print('vertices = ', vertices)
print('faces = ', faces)
```

For each vertex, we can also define properties other than the *x*, *y*, and *z* coordinates. For example, we can also define colors for each vertex. An example of `parallel_plane_color.ply` is shown here:

```
ply
format ascii 1.0
comment created for the book 3D Deep Learning with Python
element vertex 8
property float32 x
property float32 y
property float32 z
```

```
property uchar red
property uchar green
property uchar blue
element face 4
property list uint8 int32 vertex_indices
end_header
-1 -1 -1 255 0 0
1 -1 -1 255 0 0
1 1 -1 255 0 0
-1 1 -1 255 0 0
-1 -1 1 0 0 255
1 -1 1 0 0 255
1 1 1 0 0 255
-1 1 1 0 0 255
3 0 1 2
3 0 2 3
3 5 4 7
3 5 7 6
```

Note that in the preceding example, along with x, y, and z, we also define some additional properties for each vertex – that is, the red, green, and blue properties, all in the uchar data type. Now, each record for one vertex is one line of six numbers. The first three are x, y, and z coordinates. The following three numbers are the RGB values.

The mesh can be visualized by using ply_example3.py as follows:

```
import open3d
from pytorch3d.io import import load_ply

mesh_file = "parallel_plane_color.ply"
print('visualizing the mesh using open3D')
mesh = open3d.io.read_triangle_mesh(mesh_file)
open3d.visualization.draw_geometries([mesh],
                    mesh_show_wireframe = True,
                    mesh_show_back_face = True)

print("Loading the same file with PyTorch3D")
vertices, faces = load_ply(mesh_file)
```

```
print('Type of vertices = ', type(vertices), ", type of faces =
", type(faces))
print('vertices = ', vertices)
print('faces = ', faces)
```

We also provide `cow.ply`, which is a real-world example of a 3D mesh. The readers can visualize the mesh using `ply_example4.py`.

By now, we have talked about the basic elements of the PLY file format, such as vertices and faces. Next, we will discuss the OBJ 3D data format.

3D data file format – OBJ files

In this section, we are going to discuss another widely used 3D data file format, the OBJ file format. The OBJ file format was first developed by Wavefront Technologies Inc. Like the PLY file format, the OBJ format also has both an ASCII version and a binary version. The binary version is proprietary and undocumented. So, we are going to discuss the ASCII version in this section.

Like the previous section, here we are going to learn the file format by looking at examples. The first example, `cube.obj`, is shown as follows. As you can guess, the OBJ file defines a mesh of a cube.

The first line, `mtlib ./cube.mtl`, declares the companion **Material Template Library** (MTL) file. The **MTL** file describes surface shading properties, which will be explained in the next code snippet.

For the `o cube` line, the starting letter, o, indicates that the line defines an object, where the name of the object is `cube`. Any line starting with # is a comment line – that is, the rest of the line will be ignored by a computer. Each line starts with v, which indicates that each line defines a vertex. For example, `v -0.5 -0.5 0.5` defines a vertex with an *x* coordinate of 0.5, a *y* coordinate of 0.5, and a *z* coordination of 0.5. For each line starting with f, f indicates that each line contains a definition for one face. For example, the `f 1 2 3` line defines a face, with its three vertices being the vertices with indices 1, 2, and 3.

The `usemtl Door` line declares that the surfaces declared after this line should be shaded using a material property defined in the MTL file, named `Door`:

```
mtllib ./cube.mtl
o cube
# Vertex list
v -0.5 -0.5 0.5
v -0.5 -0.5 -0.5
v -0.5 0.5 -0.5
v -0.5 0.5 0.5
v 0.5 -0.5 0.5
```

```
v 0.5 -0.5 -0.5
v 0.5 0.5 -0.5
v 0.5 0.5 0.5

# Point/Line/Face list
usemtl Door

f 1 2 3
f 6 5 8
f 7 3 2
f 4 8 5
f 8 4 3
f 6 2 1
f 1 3 4
f 6 8 7
f 7 2 6
f 4 5 1
f 8 3 7
f 6 1 5
```

The cube.mtl companion MTL file is shown as follows. The file defines a material property called Door:

```
newmtl Door
Ka   0.8 0.6 0.4
Kd   0.8 0.6 0.4
Ks   0.9 0.9 0.9
d    1.0
Ns   0.0
illum 2
```

We will not discuss these material properties in detail except for map_Kd. If you are curious, you can refer to a standard computer graphics textbook such as *Computer Graphics: Principles and Practice*. We will list some rough descriptions of these properties as follows, just for the sake of completeness:

- Ka: Specifies an ambient color
- Kd: Specifies a diffuse color
- Ks: Specifies a specular color
- Ns: Defines the focus of specular highlights

- Ni: Defines the optical density (a.k.a index of refraction)

- d: Specifies a factor for dissolve

- illum: Specifies an illumination model

- map_Kd: Specifies a color texture file to be applied to the diffuse reflectivity of the material

The cube.obj file can be opened by both Open3D and PyTorch3D. The following code snippet, obj_example1.py, can be downloaded from our GitHub repository:

```
import open3d
from pytorch3d.io import import load_obj

mesh_file = "cube.obj"
print('visualizing the mesh using open3D')
mesh = open3d.io.read_triangle_mesh(mesh_file)
open3d.visualization.draw_geometries([mesh],
                mesh_show_wireframe = True,
                mesh_show_back_face = True)

print("Loading the same file with PyTorch3D")
vertices, faces, aux = load_obj(mesh_file)
print('Type of vertices = ', type(vertices))
print("Type of faces = ", type(faces))
print("Type of aux = ", type(aux))
print('vertices = ', vertices)
print('faces = ', faces)
print('aux = ', aux)
```

In the preceding code snippet, the defined mesh of a cube can be interactively visualized by using the Open3D draw_geometries function. The mesh will be shown in a window, and you can rotate, zoom into, and zoom out of the mesh using your mouse. The mesh can also be loaded using the PyTorch3D load_obj function. The load_obj function will return the vertices, faces, and aux variables, either in the format of a PyTorch tensor or tuples of PyTorch tensors.

An example output of the obj_example1.py code snippet is shown as follows:

```
visualizing the mesh using open3D
Loading the same file with PyTorch3D
Type of vertices =  <class 'torch.Tensor'>
Type of faces =  <class 'pytorch3d.io.obj_io.Faces'>
```

```
Type of aux =  <class 'pytorch3d.io.obj_io.Properties'>
vertices =  tensor([[-0.5000, -0.5000,  0.5000],
        [-0.5000, -0.5000, -0.5000],
        [-0.5000,  0.5000, -0.5000],
        [-0.5000,  0.5000,  0.5000],
        [ 0.5000, -0.5000,  0.5000],
        [ 0.5000, -0.5000, -0.5000],
        [ 0.5000,  0.5000, -0.5000],
        [ 0.5000,  0.5000,  0.5000]])
faces =  Faces(verts_idx=tensor([[0, 1, 2],
        [5, 4, 7],
        [6, 2, 1],
        ...
        [3, 4, 0],
        [7, 2, 6],
        [5, 0, 4]]), normals_idx=tensor([[-1, -1, -1],
        [-1, -1, -1],
        [-1, -1, -1],
        [-1, -1, -1],
        ...
        [-1, -1, -1],
        [-1, -1, -1]]), textures_idx=tensor([[-1, -1, -1],
        [-1, -1, -1],
        [-1, -1, -1],
        ...
        [-1, -1, -1],
        [-1, -1, -1]]), materials_idx=tensor([0, 0, 0, 0, 0, 0,
0, 0, 0, 0, 0, 0]))
aux =  Properties(normals=None, verts_uvs=None, material_
colors={'Door': {'ambient_color': tensor([0.8000, 0.6000,
0.4000]), 'diffuse_color': tensor([0.8000, 0.6000, 0.4000]),
'specular_color': tensor([0.9000, 0.9000, 0.9000]),
'shininess': tensor([0.])}}, texture_images={}, texture_
atlas=None)
```

From the code snippet output here, we know that the returned vertices variable is a PyTorch tensor with a shape of 8 x 3, where each row is a vertex with the *x*, *y*, and *z* coordinates. The returned variable, `faces`, is a named tuple of three PyTorch tensors, `verts_idx`, `normals_idx`, and `textures_idx`. In the preceding example, all the `normals_idx` and `textures_idx` tensors are invalid because `cube.obj` does not include definitions for normal and textures. We will see in the next example how normals and textures can be defined in the OBJ file format. `verts_idx` is the vertex indices for each face. Note that the vertex indices are 0-indexed here in PyTorch3D, where the indices start from 0. However, the vertex indices in OBJ files are 1-indexed, where the indices start from 1. PyTorch3D has already made the conversion between the two ways of vertex indexing for us.

The return variable, `aux`, contains some extra mesh information. Note that the `texture_image` field of the `aux` variable is empty. The texture images are used in MTL files to define colors on vertices and faces. Again, we will show how to use this feature in our next example.

In the second example, we will use an example `cube_texture.obj` file to highlight more OBJ file features. The file is shown as follows.

The `cube_texture.obj` file is like the `cube.obj` file, except for the following differences:

- There are some additional lines starting with `vt`. Each such line declares a texture vertex with *x* and *y* coordinates. Each texture vertex defines a color. The color is the pixel color at a so-called texture image, where the pixel location is the *x* coordinate of the texture vertex x width, and the *y* coordinate of the texture vertex x height. The texture image would be defined in the `cube_texture.mtl` companion.

- There are additional lines starting with `vn`. Each such line declares a normal vector – for example, the `vn 0.000000 -1.000000 0.000000` line declares a normal vector pointing to the negative *z* axis.

- Each face definition line now contains more information about each vertex. For example, the `f 2/1/1 3/2/1 4/3/1` line contains the definitions for the three vertices. The first triple, `2/1/1`, defines the first vertex, the second triple, `3/2/1`, defines the second vertex, and the third triple, `4/3/1`, defines the third vertex. Each such triplet is the vertex index, texture vertex index, and normal vector index. For example, `2/1/1` defines a vertex, where the vertex geometric location is defined in the second line starting with `v`, the color is defined in the first line starting with `vt`, and the normal vector is defined in the first line starting with `vn`:

```
mtllib cube_texture.mtl

v 1.000000 -1.000000 -1.000000
v 1.000000 -1.000000 1.000000
v -1.000000 -1.000000 1.000000
v -1.000000 -1.000000 -1.000000
v 1.000000 1.000000 -0.999999
```

```
v 0.999999 1.000000 1.000001
v -1.000000 1.000000 1.000000
v -1.000000 1.000000 -1.000000

vt 1.000000 0.333333
vt 1.000000 0.666667
vt 0.666667 0.666667
vt 0.666667 0.333333
vt 0.666667 0.000000
vt 0.000000 0.333333
vt 0.000000 0.000000
vt 0.333333 0.000000
vt 0.333333 1.000000
vt 0.000000 1.000000
vt 0.000000 0.666667
vt 0.333333 0.333333
vt 0.333333 0.666667
vt 1.000000 0.000000

vn 0.000000 -1.000000 0.000000
vn 0.000000 1.000000 0.000000
vn 1.000000 0.000000 0.000000
vn -0.000000 0.000000 1.000000
vn -1.000000 -0.000000 -0.000000
vn 0.000000 0.000000 -1.000000

g main
usemtl Skin

s 1
f 2/1/1 3/2/1 4/3/1
f 8/1/2 7/4/2 6/5/2
f 5/6/3 6/7/3 2/8/3
f 6/8/4 7/5/4 3/4/4
f 3/9/5 7/10/5 8/11/5
f 1/12/6 4/13/6 8/11/6
```

```
f 1/4/1 2/1/1 4/3/1
f 5/14/2 8/1/2 6/5/2
f 1/12/3 5/6/3 2/8/3
f 2/12/4 6/8/4 3/4/4
f 4/13/5 3/9/5 8/11/5
f 5/6/6 1/12/6 8/11/6
```

The cube_texture.mtl companion is as follows, where the line starting with map_Kd declares the texture image. Here, wal67ar_small.jpg is a 250 x 250 RGB image file in the same folder as the MTL file:

```
newmtl Skin
Ka 0.200000 0.200000 0.200000
Kd 0.827451 0.792157 0.772549
Ks 0.000000 0.000000 0.000000
Ns 0.000000
map_Kd ./wal67ar_small.jpg
```

Again, we can use Open3D and PyTorch3D to load the mesh in the cube_texture.obj file – for example, by using the following obj_example2.py file:

```
import open3d
from pytorch3d.io import load_obj
import torch

mesh_file = "cube_texture.obj"

print('visualizing the mesh using open3D')
mesh = open3d.io.read_triangle_mesh(mesh_file)
open3d.visualization.draw_geometries([mesh],
                mesh_show_wireframe = True,
                mesh_show_back_face = True)

print("Loading the same file with PyTorch3D")
vertices, faces, aux = load_obj(mesh_file)
print('Type of vertices = ', type(vertices))
print("Type of faces = ", type(faces))
print("Type of aux = ", type(aux))
```

```
print('vertices = ', vertices)
print('faces = ', faces)
print('aux = ', aux)

texture_images = getattr(aux, 'texture_images')
print('texture_images type = ', type(texture_images))
print(texture_images['Skin'].shape)
```

The output of the obj_example2.py code snippet should be as follows:

```
visualizing the mesh using open3D
Loading the same file with PyTorch3D
Type of vertices =  <class 'torch.Tensor'>
Type of faces =  <class 'pytorch3d.io.obj_io.Faces'>
Type of aux =  <class 'pytorch3d.io.obj_io.Properties'>
vertices =  tensor([[ 1.0000, -1.0000, -1.0000],
        [ 1.0000, -1.0000,  1.0000],
        [-1.0000, -1.0000,  1.0000],
        [-1.0000, -1.0000, -1.0000],
        [ 1.0000,  1.0000, -1.0000],
        [ 1.0000,  1.0000,  1.0000],
        [-1.0000,  1.0000,  1.0000],
        [-1.0000,  1.0000, -1.0000]])
faces =  Faces(verts_idx=tensor([[1, 2, 3],
        [7, 6, 5],
        [4, 5, 1],
        [5, 6, 2],
        [2, 6, 7],
        [0, 3, 7],
        [0, 1, 3],
        ...
        [3, 3, 3],
        [4, 4, 4],
        [5, 5, 5]]), textures_idx=tensor([[ 0,  1,  2],
        [ 0,  3,  4],
        [ 5,  6,  7],
        [ 7,  4,  3],
```

```
            [ 8,   9,  10],
            [11,  12,  10],
            ...
            [12,   8,  10],
            [ 5,  11,  10]]), materials_idx=tensor([0, 0, 0, 0, 0, 0,
0, 0, 0, 0, 0, 0]))
aux =  Properties(normals=tensor([[ 0.,  -1.,    0.],
            [ 0.,   1.,    0.],
            [ 1.,   0.,    0.],
            [-0.,   0.,    1.],
            [-1.,  -0.,   -0.],
            [ 0.,   0.,   -1.]]), verts_uvs=tensor([[1.0000, 0.3333],
            ...
            [0.3333, 0.6667],
            [1.0000, 0.0000]]), material_colors={'Skin': {'ambient_
color': tensor([0.2000, 0.2000, 0.2000]), 'diffuse_color':
tensor([0.8275, 0.7922, 0.7725]), 'specular_color': tensor([0.,
0., 0.]), 'shininess': tensor([0.])}}, texture_images={'Skin':
tensor([[[0.2078, 0.1765, 0.1020],
            [0.2039, 0.1725, 0.0980],
            [0.1961, 0.1647, 0.0902],
            ...,
            [0.2235, 0.1882, 0.1294]]])}, texture_atlas=None)
texture_images type =  <class 'dict'>
Skin
torch.Size([250, 250, 3])
```

> **Note**
> This is not the complete output; please check this while you run the code.

Compared with the output of the `obj_example1.py` code snippet, the preceding output has the following differences.

- The `normals_idx` and `textures_idx` fields of the `faces` variable all contain valid indices now instead of taking a -1 value.

- The `normals` field of the `aux` variable is a PyTorch tensor now, instead of being None.

- The `verts_uvs` field of the `aux` variable is a PyTorch tensor now, instead of being None.

- The `texture_images` field of the `aux` variable is not an empty dictionary any longer. The `texture_images` dictionary contains one entry with a key, `Skin`, and a PyTorch tensor with a shape of (250, 250, 3). This tensor is exactly the same as the image contained in the `wal67ar_small.jpg` file, as defined in the `mtl_texture.mtl` file.

We have learned how to use basic 3D data file formats and PLY and OBJ files. In the next section, we will learn the basic concepts of 3D coordination systems.

Understanding 3D coordination systems

In this section, we are going to learn about the frequently used coordination systems in PyTorch3D. This section is adapted from PyTorch's documentation of camera coordinate systems: `https://pytorch3d.org/docs/cameras`. To understand and use the PyTorch3D rendering system, we usually need to know these coordination systems and how to use them. As discussed in the previous sections, 3D data can be represented by points, faces, and voxels. The location of each point can be represented by a set of x, y, and z coordinates, with respect to a certain coordination system. We usually need to define and use multiple coordination systems, depending on which one is most convenient.

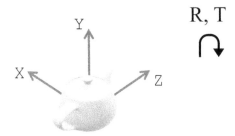

Figure 1.2 – A world coordinate system, where the origin and axis
are defined independently of the camera positions

The first coordination system we frequently use is called the **world coordination system**. This coordinate system is a 3D coordination system chosen with respect to all the 3D objects, such that the locations of the 3D objects can be easy to determine. Usually, the axis of the world coordination system does not agree with the object orientation or camera orientation. Thus, there exist some non-zero rotations and displacements between the origin of the world coordination system and the object and camera orientations. A figure showing the world coordination system is shown here:

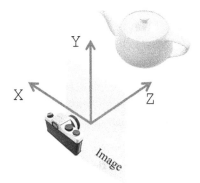

Figure 1.3 – The camera view coordinate system, where the origin is at the camera
projection center and the three axes are defined according to the imaging plane

Since the axis of the world coordination system usually does not agree with the camera orientation, for many situations, it is more convenient to define and use a camera view coordination system. In PyTorch3D, the camera view coordination system is defined such that the origin is at the projection point of the camera, the x axis points to the left, the y axis points upward, and the z axis points to the front.

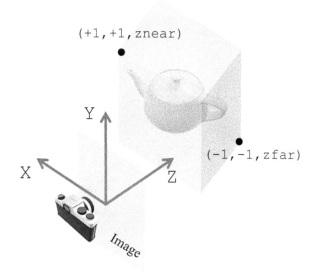

Figure 1.4 – The NDC coordinate system, in which the volume is
confined to the ranges that the camera can render

The **normalized device coordinate** (**NDC**) confines the volume that a camera can render. The x coordinate values in the NDC space range from -1 to +1, as do the y coordinate values. The z coordinate values range from znear to zfar, where znear is the nearest depth and zfar is the farthest depth. Any object out of this znear to zfar range would not be rendered by the camera.

Finally, the screen coordinate system is defined in terms of how the rendered images are shown on our screens. The coordinate system contains the x coordinate as the columns of the pixels, the y coordinate as the rows of the pixels, and the z coordinate corresponding to the depth of the object.

To render the 3D object correctly on our 2D screens, we need to switch between these coordinate systems. Luckily, these conversions can be easily carried out by using the PyTorch3D camera models. We will discuss coordinatation conversion in more detail after we discuss the camera models.

Understanding camera models

In this section, we will learn about camera models. In 3D deep learning, usually we need to use 2D images for 3D detection. Either 3D information is detected solely from 2D images, or 2D images are fused with depth for high accuracy. Nevertheless, camera models are essential to build correspondence between the 2D space and the 3D world.

In PyTorch3D, there are two major camera models, the orthographic camera defined by the OrthographicCameras class and the perspective camera model defined by the PerspectiveCameras class. The following figure shows the differences between the two camera models.

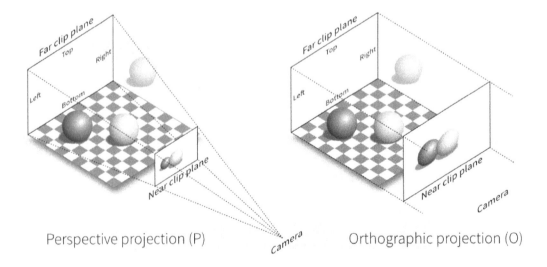

Figure 1.5 – Two major camera models implemented in PyTorch3D, perspective and orthographic

The orthographic cameras use orthographic projections to map objects in the 3D world to 2D images, while the perspective cameras use perspective projections to map objects in the 3D world to 2D images. The orthographic projections map objects to 2D images, disregarding the object depth. For example, just as shown in the figure, two objects with the same geometric size at different depths would be mapped to 2D images of the same size. On the other hand, in perspective projections, if an object moved far away from the camera, it would be mapped to a smaller size on the 2D images.

Now that we have learned about the basic concept of camera models, let us look at some coding examples to see how we can create and use these camera models.

Coding for camera models and coordination systems

In this section, we are going to leverage everything we have learned to build a concrete camera model and convert between different coordinate systems, using a concrete code snippet example written in Python and PyTorch3D:

1. First, we are going to use the following mesh defined by a cube.obj file. Basically, the mesh is a cube:

```
mtllib ./cube.mtl
o cube
# Vertex list
v -50 -50 20
v -50 -50 10
v -50 50 10
v -50 50 20
v 50 -50 20
v 50 -50 10
v 50 50 10
v 50 50 20

# Point/Line/Face list
usemtl Door

f 1 2 3
f 6 5 8
f 7 3 2
f 4 8 5
f 8 4 3
f 6 2 1
```

```
f 1 3 4
f 6 8 7
f 7 2 6
f 4 5 1
f 8 3 7
f 6 1 5
# End of file
```

The example code snippet is `camera.py`, which can be downloaded from the book's GitHub repository.

2. Let us import all the modules that we need:

```
import open3d
import torch
import pytorch3d
from pytorch3d.io import load_obj
from scipy.spatial.transform import Rotation as Rotation

from pytorch3d.renderer.cameras import PerspectiveCameras
```

3. We can load and visualize the mesh by using Open3D's `draw_geometrics` function:

```
#Load meshes and visualize it with Open3D
mesh_file = "cube.obj"
print('visualizing the mesh using open3D')
mesh = open3d.io.read_triangle_mesh(mesh_file)
open3d.visualization.draw_geometries([mesh],
                mesh_show_wireframe = True,
                mesh_show_back_face = True)
```

4. We define a `camera` variable as a PyTorch3D `PerspectiveCamera` object. The camera here is actually mini-batched. For example, the rotation matrix, R, is a PyTorch tensor with a shape of [8, 3, 3], which actually defines eight cameras, each with one of the eight rotation matrices. This is the same case for all other camera parameters, such as image sizes, focal lengths, and principal points:

```
#Define a mini-batch of 8 cameras
image_size = torch.ones(8, 2)
image_size[:,0] = image_size[:,0] * 1024
```

```
image_size[:,1] = image_size[:,1] * 512
image_size = image_size.cuda()


focal_length = torch.ones(8, 2)
focal_length[:,0] = focal_length[:,0] * 1200
focal_length[:,1] = focal_length[:,1] * 300
focal_length = focal_length.cuda()


principal_point = torch.ones(8, 2)
principal_point[:,0] = principal_point[:,0] * 512
principal_point[:,1] = principal_point[:,1] * 256
principal_point = principal_point.cuda()


R = Rotation.from_euler('zyx', [
    [n*5, n, n]  for n in range(-4, 4, 1)],
degrees=True).as_matrix()
R = torch.from_numpy(R).cuda()
T = [ [n, 0, 0] for n in range(-4, 4, 1)]
T = torch.FloatTensor(T).cuda()


camera = PerspectiveCameras(focal_length = focal_length,
                            principal_point = principal_
point,
                            in_ndc = False,
                            image_size = image_size,
                            R = R,
                            T = T,
                            device = 'cuda')
```

5. Once we have defined the camera variable, we can call the get_world_to_view_transform class member method to obtain a Transform3d object, world_to_view_transform. We can then use the transform_points member method to convert from world coordination to camera view coordination. Similarly, we can also use the get_full_projection_transform member method to obtain a Transform3d object, which is for the conversion from world coordination to screen coordination:

```
world_to_view_transform = camera.get_world_to_view_
transform()
```

```
world_to_screen_transform = camera.get_full_projection_
transform()

#Load meshes using PyTorch3D
vertices, faces, aux = load_obj(mesh_file)
vertices = vertices.cuda()

world_to_view_vertices = world_to_view_transform.
transform_points(vertices)
world_to_screen_vertices = world_to_screen_transform.
transform_points(vertices)

print('world_to_view_vertices = ', world_to_view_
vertices)
print('world_to_screen_vertices = ', world_to_screen_
vertices
```

The code example shows the basic ways that PyTorch3D cameras can be used and how easy it is to switch between different coordinate systems using PyTorch3D.

Summary

In this chapter, we first learned how to set up our development environment. We then talked about the most widely used 3D data representations. We then explored some concrete examples of 3D data representation by learning about the 3D data file formats, the PLY format and the OBJ format. Then, we learned about the basic concepts of 3D coordination systems and camera models. In the last part of the chapter, we learned how to build camera models and convert between different coordination systems through a hands-on coding example.

In the next chapter, we will talk about more important 3D deep learning concepts, such as rendering to convert 3D models to 2D images, heterogeneous mini-batching, and several ways to represent rotations.

2

Introducing 3D Computer Vision and Geometry

In this chapter, we will learn about some basic concepts of 3D computer vision and geometry that will be especially useful for later chapters in this book. We will start by discussing what rendering, rasterization, and shading are. We will go through different lighting models and shading models, such as point light sources, directional light sources, ambient lighting, diffusion, highlights, and shininess. We will go through a coding example for rendering a mesh model using different lighting models and parameters.

We will then learn how to use PyTorch for solving optimization problems. Particularly, we will go through stochastic gradient descent over heterogeneous mini-batches, which becomes possible by using PyTorch3D. We will also learn about different formats for mini-batches in PyTorch3D, including the list, padded, and packed formats, and learn how to convert between the different formats.

In the last part of the chapter, we will discuss some frequently used rotation representations and how to convert between these representations.

In this chapter, we're going to cover the following topics:

- Exploring the basic concepts of rendering, rasterization, and shading
- Understanding the Lambertian shading and Phong shading models
- How to define a PyTorch tensor and optimize the tensor using an optimizer
- How to define a mini-batch and heterogeneous mini-batch and packed and padded tensors
- Rotations and different ways to describe rotations
- Exponential mapping and log mapping in the SE(3) space

Technical requirements

To run the example code snippets in this book, the readers need to have a computer, ideally with a GPU. However, running the code snippets only with CPUs is not impossible.

The recommended computer configuration includes the following:

- A modern GPU – for example, the Nvidia GTX series or RTX series with at least 8 GB of memory
- Python 3
- PyTorch library and PyTorch3D libraries

The code snippets with this chapter can be found at `https://github.com/PacktPublishing/3D-Deep-Learning-with-Python`.

Exploring the basic concepts of rendering, rasterization, and shading

Rendering is a process that takes 3D data models of the world around our camera as input and output images. It is an approximation to the physical process where images are formed in our camera in the real world. Typically, the 3D data models are meshes. In this case, rendering is usually done using ray tracing:

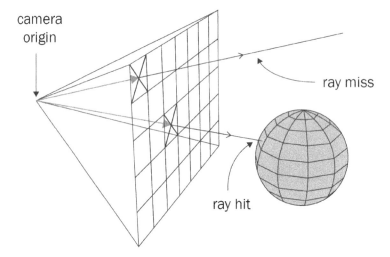

Figure 2.1: Rendering by ray tracing (rays are generated from camera origins and go through the image pixels for finding relevant mesh faces)

An example of ray tracing processing is shown in *Figure 2.1*. In the example, the world model contains one 3D sphere, which is represented by a mesh model. To form the image of the 3D sphere, for each image pixel, we generate one ray, starting from the camera origin and going through the image pixel. If one ray intersects with one mesh face, then we know the mesh face can project its color to the image pixel. We also need to trace the depth of each intersection because a face with a smaller depth would occlude faces with larger depths.

Thus, the process of rendering can usually be divided into two stages – rasterization and shading. The ray tracing process is a typical rasterization process – that is, the process of finding relevant geometric objects for each image pixel. Shading is the process of taking the outputs of the rasterization and computing the pixel value for each image pixel.

The `pytorch3d.renderer.mesh.rasterize_meshes.rasterize_meshes` function in PyTorch3D usually computes the following four things for each image pixel:

- `pix_to_face` is a list of face indices that the ray may intersect.
- `zbuf` is a list of depth values of these faces.
- `bary_coords` is a list of barycentric coordinates of the intersection point of each face and the ray.
- `pix_dists` is a list of signed distances between pixels (*x* and *y*) and the nearest point on all the faces where the ray intersects. The values of this list can take negative values since it contains signed distances.

Note that usually, one face with the smallest depth would occlude all the mesh faces with larger depths. Thus, if all we need is the rendered image, then all we need in this list is the face with the smallest depth. However, with the more advanced setting of differentiable rendering (which we will cover in later chapters of this book), the pixel colors are usually fused from multiple mesh faces.

Understanding barycentric coordinates

For each point coplanar with a mesh face, the coordinates of the point can always be written as a linear combination of the coordinates of the three vertices of the mesh face. For example, as shown in the following diagram, the point p can be written as $uA + vB + wC$, where A, B, and C are the coordinates of the three vertices of the mesh face. Thus, we can represent each such point with the coefficients u, v, and w. This representation is called the barycentric coordinates of the point. For point lays within the mesh face triangle, $u + v + w = 1$ and all u,v,w are positive numbers. Since barycentric coordinates define any point inside a face as a function of face vertices, we can use the same coefficients to interpolate other properties across the whole face as a function of the properties defined at the vertices of the face. For example, we can use it for shading as shown in *Figure 2.2*:

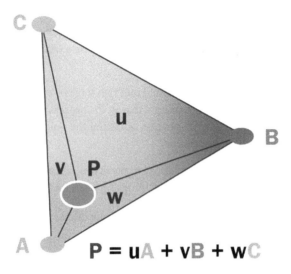

Figure 2.2: Definition of the barycentric coordinate system

Once we have a list of the `pix_to_face`, `zbuf`, `bary_coords`, and `dists` values, a shading process would mimic the physical process of image formation as in the real world. Thus, we are going to discuss several physical models for color formation.

Light source models

Light propagation in the real world can be a sophisticated process. Several approximations of light sources are usually used in shading to reduce computational costs:

- The first assumption is ambient lighting, where we assume that there is some background light radiation after sufficient reflections, such that they usually come from all directions with almost the same amplitude at all image pixels.

- Another assumption that we usually use is that some light sources can be considered point light sources. A point light source radiates lights from one single point and the radiations at all directions have the same color and amplitude.

- A third assumption that we usually use is that some light sources can be modeled as directional light sources. In such a case, the light directions from the light source are identical at all the 3D spatial locations. Directional lighting is a good approximation model for cases where the light sources are far away from the rendered objects – for example, sunlight.

Understanding the Lambertian shading model

The first physical model that we will discuss is Lambert's cosine law. Lambertian surfaces are types of objects that are not shiny at all, such as paper, unfinished wood, and unpolished stones:

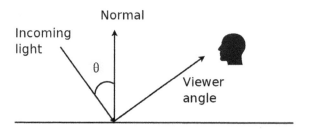

Figure 2.3: Light diffusion on Lambertian surfaces

Figure 2.3 shows an example of how lights diffuse on a Lambertian surface. One basic idea of the Lambertian cosine law is that for Lambertian surfaces, the amplitude of the reflected light does not depend on the viewer's angle, but only depends on the angle θ between the surface normal and the direction of the incident light. More precisely, the intensity of the reflected light c is as follows:

$$c = c_r c_l \cos(\theta)$$

Here, c_r is the material's reflected coefficient and c_l is the amplitude of the incident light. If we further consider the ambient light, the amplitude of the reflected light is as follows:

$$c = c_r(c_a + c_l \cos(\theta))$$

Here, c_a is the amplitude of the ambient light.

Understanding the Phong lighting model

For shiny surfaces, such as polished tile floors and glossy paint, the reflected light also contains a highlight component. The Phong lighting model is a frequently used model for these glossy components:

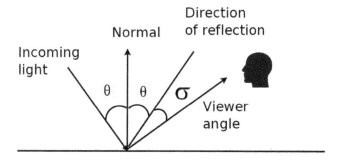

Figure 2.4: The Phong lighting model

An example of the Phong lighting model is shown in *Figure 2.4*. One basic principle of the Phong lighting model is that the shiny light component should be strongest in the direction of reflection of the incoming light. The component would become weaker as the angle C between the direction of reflection and the viewing angle becomes larger.

More precisely, the amplitude of the shiny light component c is equal to the following:

$$c = c_r c_l c_p [cos(\sigma)]^p$$

Here, the exponent p is a parameter of the model for controlling the speed at which the shiny components attenuate when the viewing angle is away from the direction of reflection.

Finally, if we consider all three major components – ambient lighting, diffusion, and highlights – the final equation for the amplitude of light is as follows:

$$c = c_r\big(c_a + c_l\,cos(\theta) + c_l c_p [cos(\sigma)]^p\big)$$

Note that the preceding equation applies to each color component. In other words, we will have one of these equations for each color channel (red, green, and blue) with a distinct set of c_r, c_a, c_l values:

Now, we have learned about the basic concepts of rendering, rasterization, and rendering. We have also learned about the different light source models and shading models. We are ready to perform some coding exercises to use these light sources and shading models.

Coding exercises for 3D rendering

In this section, we will look at a concrete coding exercise using PyTorch3D for rendering a mesh model. We are going to learn how to define a camera model and how to define a light source in PyTorch3D. We will also learn how to change the incoming light components and material properties so that more realistic images can be rendered by controlling the three light components (ambient, diffusion, and glossy):

1. First, we need to import all the Python modules that we need:

    ```
    import open3d
    import os
    import sys
    import torch

    import matplotlib.pyplot as plt
    from pytorch3d.io import load_objs_as_meshes
    from pytorch3d.renderer import (
        look_at_view_transform,
        PerspectiveCameras,
    ```

```
        PerspectiveCameras,
        PointLights,
        Materials,
        RasterizationSettings,
        MeshRenderer,
        MeshRasterizer
    )


    from pytorch3d.renderer.mesh.shader import
    HardPhongShader


    sys.path.append(os.path.abspath(''))
```

2. Then, we need to load the mesh that we are going to use. The `cow.obj` file contains a mesh model for a toy cow object:

```
DATA_DIR = "./data"
obj_filename = os.path.join(DATA_DIR, "cow_mesh/cow.obj")
device = torch.device('cuda')
mesh = load_objs_as_meshes([obj_filename], device=device)
```

3. We will define the cameras and light sources next. We use the `look_at_view_transform` function to map easy-to-understand parameters, such as the distance from the camera, elevation angle, and azimuth angle to obtain the rotation (R) and translation (T) matrices. The R and T variables define where we are going to place our camera. The `lights` variable is a point light source placed at `[0.0, 0.0, -3.0]` as its location:

```
R, T = look_at_view_transform(2.7, 0, 180)
cameras = PerspectiveCameras(device=device, R=R, T=T)


lights = PointLights(device=device, location=[[0.0, 0.0,
-3.0]])
```

4. We will define a `renderer` variable of the `MeshRenderer` type. A `renderer` variable is a callable object, which can take a mesh as input and output the rendered images. Note that the renderer takes two inputs in its initialization – one rasterizer and one shader. PyTorch3D has defined several different types of rasterizers and shaders. Here, we are going to use `MeshRasterizer` and `HardPhongShader`. Note that we can also specify the setting of the rasterizer. `image_size` is equal to `512` here, which implies the rendered images would be 512 x 512 pixels. `blur_radius` is set to 0 and `faces_per_pixel` is set to 1.

The `blur_radius` and `faces_per_pixel` settings are the most useful for differentiable rendering, where `blur_radius` should be greater than 0 and `faces_per_pixel` should be greater than 1:

```
raster_settings = RasterizationSettings(
    image_size=512,
    blur_radius=0.0,
    faces_per_pixel=1,
)


renderer = MeshRenderer(
    rasterizer=MeshRasterizer(
        cameras=cameras,
        raster_settings=raster_settings
    ),
    shader = HardPhongShader(
        device = device,
        cameras = cameras,
        lights = lights
    )
)
```

5. We are therefore ready to run our first rendering results by calling the renderer and passing the mesh model. The rendered image is shown in *Figure 2.5*:

```
images = renderer(mesh)
plt.figure(figsize=(10, 10))
plt.imshow(images[0, ..., :3].cpu().numpy())
plt.axis("off")
plt.savefig('light_at_front.png')
plt.show()
```

Figure 2.5: The rendered image when the light source is placed in front

6. Next, we will change the location of the light source to the back of the mesh and see what will happen. The rendered image is shown in *Figure 2.6*. In this case, the light from the point light source cannot intersect with any mesh faces that are facing us. Thus, all the colors that we can observe here are due to ambient light:

```
lights.location = torch.tensor([0.0, 0.0, +1.0],
device=device)[None]
images = renderer(mesh, lights=lights, )
plt.figure(figsize=(10, 10))
plt.imshow(images[0, ..., :3].cpu().numpy())
plt.axis("off")
plt.savefig('light_at_back.png')
plt.show()
```

Figure 2.6: The rendered image when the light source is placed behind the toy cow

7.   In the next experiment, we are going to define a materials data structure. Here, we change the configuration so that the ambient components are close to 0 (indeed, being 0.01). Because the point light source is behind the object and the ambient light is also turned off, the rendered object does not reflect any light now. The rendered image is shown in *Figure 2.7*:

```
materials = Materials(
    device=device,
    specular_color=[[0.0, 1.0, 0.0]],
    shininess=10.0,
    ambient_color=((0.01, 0.01, 0.01),),
)
images = renderer(mesh, lights=lights, materials = materials)
```

```
plt.figure(figsize=(10, 10))
plt.imshow(images[0, ..., :3].cpu().numpy())
plt.axis("off")
plt.savefig('dark.png')
plt.show()
```

Figure 2.7: The rendered image without ambient light and the point light source behind the toy cow

8.   In the next experiment, we will rotate the camera again and redefine the light source location so that the light can shine on the cow's face. Note that when we define the material, we set shininess to 10.0. This shininess parameter is precisely the p parameter in the Phong lighting model. specular_color is [0.0, 1.0, 0.0], which implies that the surface is shiny mainly in the green component. The rendered results are shown in *Figure 2.8*:

```
R, T = look_at_view_transform(dist=2.7, elev=10, azim=-
150)
cameras = PerspectiveCameras(device=device, R=R, T=T)

lights.location = torch.tensor([[2.0, 2.0, -2.0]],
device=device)

materials = Materials(
    device=device,
    specular_color=[[0.0, 1.0, 0.0]],
    shininess=10.0
)

images = renderer(mesh, lights=lights,
materials=materials, cameras=cameras)
plt.figure(figsize=(10, 10))
plt.imshow(images[0, ..., :3].cpu().numpy())
plt.axis("off")
plt.savefig('green.png')
plt.show()
```

Figure 2.8: The rendered image with specular lighting components

9. In the next experiment, we are going to change `specular_color` to `red` and increase the shininess value. The results are shown in *Figure 2.9*:

```
materials = Materials(
    device=device,
    specular_color=[[1.0, 0.0, 0.0]],
    shininess=20.0
)

images = renderer(mesh, lights=lights,
materials=materials, cameras=cameras)
plt.figure(figsize=(10, 10))
plt.imshow(images[0, ..., :3].cpu().numpy())
plt.savefig('red.png')
plt.axis("off")
plt.show()
```

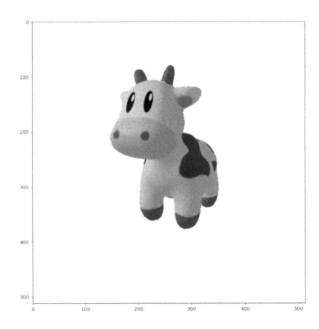

Figure 2.9: The rendered image with a red specular color

10. Finally, we turn off the shininess and the results are shown in *Figure 2.10*:

```
materials = Materials(
    device=device,
    specular_color=[[0.0, 0.0, 0.0]],
    shininess=0.0
)

images = renderer(mesh, lights=lights,
materials=materials, cameras=cameras)
plt.figure(figsize=(10, 10))
plt.imshow(images[0, ..., :3].cpu().numpy())
plt.savefig('blue.png')
plt.axis("off")
plt.show()
```

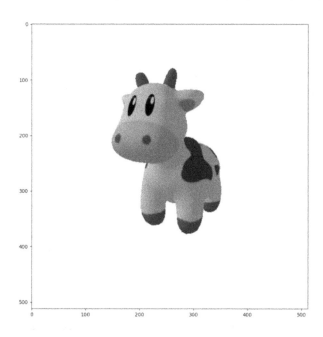

Figure 2.10: The rendered image without specular components

In the first part of this chapter, we mainly discussed rendering and shading, which are super important for 3D computer vision. Next, we will discuss another very important topic for 3D deep learning, which is the heterogeneous batch issue for optimization.

Using PyTorch3D heterogeneous batches and PyTorch optimizers

In this section, we are going to learn how to use the PyTorch optimizer on PyTorch3D heterogeneous mini-batches. In deep learning, we are usually given a list of data examples, such as the following ones – $\{(x_1, y_1), (x_2, y_2), (x_3, y_3), \dots, (x_n, y_n)\}$. Here, x_i are the observations and y_i are the prediction values. For example, x_i may be some images and y_i the ground-truth classification results – for example, "cat" or "dog". A deep neural network is then trained so that the outputs of the neural networks are as close to y_i as possible. Usually, a loss function between the neural network outputs and y_i is defined so that the loss function values decrease as the neural network outputs become closer to y_i.

Thus, training a deep learning network is usually done by minimizing the loss function that is evaluated on all training data examples, x_i and y_i. A straightforward method used in many optimization algorithms is computing the gradients first, as shown in the following equation, and then modifying the parameters of the neural network along the direction of the negative gradient. In the equation, f represents the neural network that takes x_i as its input and has parameters Θ; loss is the loss function between the neural network outputs and the ground-truth prediction y_i:

$$\frac{\partial \sum_{i=1}^{n} \text{loss}(f(x_i; \theta), y_i)}{\partial \theta}$$

However, computing this gradient is expensive, as the computational cost is proportional to the size of the training dataset. In reality, a **Stochastic Gradient Descent** (**SGD**) algorithm is used instead of the original gradient descent algorithm. In the SGD algorithm, the descent direction is computed as in the following equation:

$$\frac{\partial \sum_{k \in D} \text{loss}(f(x_k; \theta), y_k)}{\partial \theta}$$

In the equation, the so-called mini-batch D is a small subset of all the training data examples. The mini-batch D is randomly sampled from the whole training data examples in each iteration. The SGD algorithm has a much lower computational cost than the gradient descent algorithm. Due to the law of large numbers, the computed descent directions in SGD are approximately close to the gradient descent directions. It is also widely believed that SGD introduces certain implicit regularization, which may contribute to the nice generalization properties of deep learning. The method for choosing the size of the mini-batch is an important hyperparameter that needs to be considered carefully. Nevertheless, the SGD algorithm and its variants have been the methods of choice for training deep learning models.

For many data types, such as images, the data can easily be made homogeneous. We can form a mini-batch of images all with the same widths, heights, and channels. For example, a mini-batch of eight images with three channels (the three colors red, green, and blue), a height of 256, and a width of 256 can be made into a PyTorch tensor with the dimensions 8 x 3 x 256 x 256. Usually, the first dimension of the tensor represents the data sample indices within the mini-batch. Usually, computations on this kind of homogeneous data can be done efficiently using GPUs.

On the other hand, 3D data is usually heterogeneous. For example, meshes within one mini-batch may contain different numbers of vertices and faces. Processing this heterogeneous data on GPUs efficiently is not a trivial issue. Coding for the heterogeneous mini-batch processing can also be tedious. Luckily, PyTorch3D has the capacity to handle heterogeneous mini-batches very efficiently. We will go over a coding exercise involving these PyTorch3D capacities in the next section.

A coding exercise for a heterogeneous mini-batch

In this section, we are going to learn how to use the PyTorch optimizer and PyTorch3D heterogeneous mini-batch capacities by looking at a toy example. In this example, we will consider a problem where a depth camera is placed at an unknown location and we want to estimate the unknown location using the sensing results of the camera. To simplify the problem, we assume that the orientation of the camera is known and the only unknown is the 3D displacement.

More specifically, we assume that the camera observes three objects in the scene and we know the ground-truth mesh models of the three objects. Let us look at the code using PyTorch and PyTorch3D to solve the problem as follows:

1. In the first step, we are going to import all the packages that we are going to use:

    ```
    import open3d
    import os
    import torch

    from pytorch3d.io import load_objs_as_meshes
    from pytorch3d.structures.meshes import join_meshes_as_
    batch

    from pytorch3d.ops import sample_points_from_meshes
    from pytorch3d.loss import chamfer_distance
    import numpy as np
    ```

2. In the next step, we will define a `torch` device using either a CPU or CUDA:

    ```
    if torch.cuda.is_available():
        device = torch.device("cuda:0")
    else:
        device = torch.device("cpu")
        print("WARNING: CPU only, this will be slow!")
    ```

3. The mesh models that you are going to use in this toy example are included in the code repository and are under the `data` subfolder. We are going to use three mesh models contained in the

cube.obj, diamond.obj and dodecahedron.obj files. In the following code snippet, we are using the Open3D library to load these mesh models and visualize them:

```
mesh_names = ['cube.obj', 'diamond.obj', 'dodecahedron.
obj']
data_path = './data'

for mesh_name in mesh_names:
    mesh = open3d.io.read_triangle_mesh(os.path.
join(data_path, mesh_name))
    open3d.visualization.draw_geometries([mesh],
                                        mesh_show_wireframe =
True,
                                        mesh_show_back_face =
True,
                                        )
```

4. Next, we are going to use PyTorch3D to load the same meshes and build a list of meshes, which is the mesh_list variable:

```
mesh_list = list()
device = torch.device('cuda')
for mesh_name in mesh_names:
    mesh = load_objs_as_meshes([os.path.join(data_path,
mesh_name)], device=device)
    mesh_list.append(mesh)
```

5. Finally, we can create a PyTorch3D mini-batch of meshes by using the join_meshes_as_batch PyTorch3D function. The function takes a list of meshes and returns a mini-batch of meshes:

```
mesh_batch = join_meshes_as_batch(mesh_list, include_
textures = False)
```

In each PyTorch3D mini-batch, there are three ways to represent vertices and faces:

- **List format**: The vertices are represented by a list of tensors where each tensor represents the vertices or faces of one mesh within the mini-batch.

- **Padded format**: All the vertices are represented by one tensor and the data of the smaller meshes are zero-padded so that all the meshes now have the same numbers of vertices and faces.

- **Packed format**: All the vertices or faces are packed into one tensor. For each vertex or face, which mesh it belongs to is tracked internally.

The three representations all have their pros and cons. Nevertheless, the formats can be converted between each other efficiently by using the PyTorch3D API.

6. The next code snippet shows an example of how to return vertices and faces in a list format from a mini-batch:

```
vertex_list = mesh_batch.verts_list()
print('vertex_list = ', vertex_list)
face_list = mesh_batch.faces_list()
print('face_list = ', face_list)
```

7. To return vertices and faces in the padded format, we can use the following PyTorch3D API:

```
vertex_padded = mesh_batch.verts_padded()
print('vertex_padded = ', vertex_padded)
face_padded = mesh_batch.faces_padded()
print('face_padded = ', face_padded)
```

8. To get vertices and faces in the packed format, we can use the following code snippet:

```
vertex_packed = mesh_batch.verts_packed()
print('vertex_packed = ', vertex_packed)
face_packed = mesh_batch.faces_packed()
print('face_packed = ', face_packed)

num_vertices = vertex_packed.shape[0]
print('num_vertices = ', num_vertices)
```

9. In this coding example, we consider the mesh_batch variable as the ground-truth mesh model for the three objects. We will then simulate a noisy and displaced version of the three meshes. In the first step, we want to clone the ground truth mesh models:

```
mesh_batch_noisy = mesh_batch.clone()
```

10. We then define a motion_gt variable to represent the displacement between the camera location and the origin:

```
motion_gt = np.array([3, 4, 5])
motion_gt = torch.as_tensor(motion_gt)
print('motion ground truth = ', motion_gt)

motion_gt = motion_gt[None, :]
motion_gt = motion_gt.to(device)
```

11. To simulate the noisy depth camera observations, we generate some random Gaussian noise with a mean equal to motion_gt. The noises are added to mesh_batch_noisy using the offset_verts PyTorch3D function:

```
noise = (0.1**0.5)*torch.randn(mesh_batch_noisy.verts_
packed().shape).to(device)
motion_gt = np.array([3, 4, 5])
motion_gt = torch.as_tensor(motion_gt)
noise = noise + motion_gt
mesh_batch_noisy = mesh_batch_noisy.offset_verts(noise).
detach()
```

12. To estimate the unknown displacement between the camera and the origin, we will formulate an optimization problem. First, we will define the motion_estimate optimization variable. The torch.zeros function will create an all zero PyTorch tensor. Note that we set requires_grad to true. What that means is that when we run gradient backpropagation from the loss function, we want the gradient for this variable to be automatically computed by PyTorch for us:

```
motion_estimate = torch.zeros(motion_gt.shape, device =
device, requires_grad=True)
```

13. Next, we are going to define a PyTorch optimizer with a learning rate of 0.1. By passing a list of variables to the optimizer, we specify the optimization variables for this optimization problem. Here, the optimization variable is the motion_estimate variable:

```
optimizer = torch.optim.SGD([motion_estimate], lr=0.1,
momentum=0.9)
```

14. The major optimization procedure is then shown as follows. Basically, we run the stochastic gradient descent for 200 iterations. The resulting motion_estimate should be very close to the ground truth after the 200 iterations.

Each optimization iteration can be divided into the following four steps:

I.   In the first step, optimizer.zero_grad() resets all the gradient values from the values computed in the last iteration to zero.

II. In the second step, we compute the loss function. Note that PyTorch retains a dynamic computational graph. In other words, all the computation procedures toward the loss function are recorded and will be used in the backpropagation.

III. In the third step, loss.backward() computes all the gradients from the loss function to the optimization variables in the PyTorch optimizer.

IV.   In the fourth and final step, `optimizer.step` moves all the optimization variables one step in the direction of decreasing the `loss` function.

In the process of computing the `loss` function, we randomly sample 5,000 points from the two meshes and compute their Chamfer distances. The Chamfer distance is a distance between two sets of points. We will have a more detailed discussion of this distance function in later chapters:

```
for i in range(0, 200):
    optimizer.zero_grad()
    current_mesh_batch = mesh_batch.offset_verts(motion_
estimate.repeat(num_vertices,1))

    sample_trg = sample_points_from_meshes(current_mesh_batch,
5000)
    sample_src = sample_points_from_meshes(mesh_batch_noisy,
5000)
    loss, _ = chamfer_distance(sample_trg, sample_src)

    loss.backward()
    optimizer.step()
    print('i = ', i, ', motion_estimation = ', motion_estimate)
```

We can check that the optimization process here would converge to the [3,4,5] ground-truth location very quickly.

In this coding exercise, we learned how to use heterogenous mini-batches in PyTorch3D. Next, we will discuss another important concept in 3D computer vision.

Understanding transformations and rotations

In 3D deep learning and computer vision, we usually need to work with 3D transformations, such as rotations and 3D rigid motions. PyTorch3D provides a high-level encapsulation of these transformations in its `pytorch3d.transforms.Transform3d` class. One advantage of the `Transform3d` class is that it is mini-batch based. Thus, as frequently needed in 3D deep learning, it is possible to apply a mini-batch of transformations on a mini-batch of meshes only within several lines of code. Another advantage of `Transform3d` is that gradient backpropagation can straightforwardly pass through `Transform3d`.

PyTorch3D also provides many lower-level APIs for computations in the Lie groups SO(3) and SE(3). Here, SO(3) denotes the special orthogonal group in 3D and SE(3) denotes the special Euclidean group in 3D. Informally speaking, SO(3) denotes the set of all the rotation transformations and SE(3) denotes the set of all the rigid transformations in 3D. Many low-level APIs on SE(3) and SO(3) are provided in PyTorch3D.

In 3D computer vision, multiple representations exist for rotations. One representation is the rotation matrices Rx.

In this equation, x is a 3D vector and R is a 3 x 3 matrix. To be a rotation matrix, R needs to be an orthogonal matrix and has a determinant of +1. Thus, not all 3 x 3 matrices can be a rotation matrix. The degree of freedom for rotation matrices is 3.

A 3D rotation can also be represented by a 3D vector v, where the direction of v is the rotation axis. That is, the rotation would keep v fixed and rotate all the other things around v. It is also conventional to use the amplitude of v to represent the angle of rotation.

There are various mathematical connections between the two representations of rotation. If we consider a constant speed rotation around the axis v, then the rotation matrices become a matrix-valued function of the time t, $R(t)$. In this case, the gradient of $R(t)$ is always a skew-symmetric matrix, in the form shown in the following equation:

$$\begin{bmatrix} 0 & -v_z & v_y \\ v_z & 0 & -v_x \\ -v_y & v_x & 0 \end{bmatrix}$$

Here, the following applies:

$$v = \begin{bmatrix} v_x & v_y & v_z \end{bmatrix}^T$$

As we can see from these two equations, the skew-symmetric matrix of the gradient is uniquely determined by the vector v and vice versa. This mapping from the vector v to its skew-symmetric matrix form is usually called the hat operator.

A closed-form formula from the skew-symmetric matrix gradient to the rotation matrix exists as follows. The mapping is called the exponential map for $SO(3)$:

$$R = exp(A) = \sum_{n=0}^{\infty} \frac{A^n}{n!}$$

Certainly, the inverse mapping of the exponential map also exists:

$$A = log(R)$$

The mapping is called the logarithmic map for $SO(3)$.

All the hat, inverse hat, exponential, and logarithmic operations have already been implemented in PyTorch3D. PyTorch3D also implements many other frequently used 3D operations, such as quaternion operations and Euler angles.

A coding exercise for transformation and rotation

In this section, we will go through a coding exercise on how to use some of PyTorch3D's low-level APIs:

1. We begin by importing the necessary packages:

```
import torch
from pytorch3d.transforms.so3 import so3_exp_map, so3_
log_map, hat_inv, hat
```

2. We then define a PyTorch device using either a CPU or CUDA:

```
if torch.cuda.is_available():
    device = torch.device("cuda:0")
else:
    device = torch.device("cpu")
    print("WARNING: CPU only, this will be slow!")
```

3. Next, we will define a mini-batch of four rotations. Here, each rotation is represented by one 3D vector. The direction of the vector represents the rotation axis and the amplitude of the vector represents the angle of rotation:

```
log_rot = torch.zeros([4, 3], device = device)
log_rot[0, 0] = 0.001
log_rot[0, 1] = 0.0001
log_rot[0, 2] = 0.0002

log_rot[1, 0] = 0.0001
log_rot[1, 1] = 0.001
log_rot[1, 2] = 0.0002

log_rot[2, 0] = 0.0001
log_rot[2, 1] = 0.0002
log_rot[2, 2] = 0.001

log_rot[3, 0] = 0.001
log_rot[3, 1] = 0.002
log_rot[3, 2] = 0.003
```

4. The shape of `log_rot` is `[4, 3]`, where 4 is the batch size and each rotation is represented by a 3D vector. We can use the hat operator in PyTorch3D to convert them into the 3 x 3 skew-symmetric matrix representation as follows:

```
log_rot_hat = hat(log_rot)
print('log_rot_hat shape = ', log_rot_hat.shape)
print('log_rot_hat = ', log_rot_hat)
```

5. The backward conversion from the skew-symmetric matrix form to the 3D vector form is also possible using the `hat_inv` operator:

```
log_rot_copy = hat_inv(log_rot_hat)
print('log_rot_copy shape = ', log_rot_copy.shape)
print('log_rot_copy = ', log_rot_copy)
```

6. From the gradient matrix, we can compute the rotation matrix by using the PyTorch3D `so3_exp_map` function:

```
rotation_matrices = so3_exp_map(log_rot)
print('rotation_matrices = ', rotation_matrices)
```

7. The inverse conversation is `so3_log_map`, which would map the rotation matrix back to the gradient matrix again:

```
log_rot_again = so3_log_map(rotation_matrices)
print('log_rot_again = ', log_rot_again)
```

These coding exercises show the most frequently used PyTorch3D APIs for transformations and rotations. These APIs can be very useful for real-world 3D computer vision projects.

Summary

In this chapter, we learned about the basic concepts of rendering, rasterization, and shading, including light source models, the Lambertian shading model, and the Phong lighting model. We learned how to implement rendering, rasterization, and shading using PyTorch3D. We also learned how to change the parameters in the rendering process, such as ambient lighting, shininess, and specular colors, and how these parameters would affect the rendering results.

We then learned how to use the PyTorch optimizer. We went through a coding example, where the PyTorch optimizer was used on a PyTorch3D mini-batch. In the last part of the chapter, we learned how to use the PyTorch3D APIs for converting between the different representations or rotations and transformations.

In the next chapter, we will learn some more advanced techniques for using deformable mesh models for fitting real-world 3D data.

PART 2: 3D Deep Learning Using PyTorch3D

This part will cover some basic 3D computer vision processing using PyTorch3D. Implementing these 3D computer vision algorithms may become easier by using PyTorch3D. The readers will get a lot of hands-on experience working with meshes, point clouds, and fitting from images.

This part includes the following chapters:

- *Chapter 3, Fitting Deformable Mesh Models to Raw Point Clouds*
- *Chapter 4, Learning Object Pose Detection and Tracking by Differentiable Rendering*
- *Chapter 5, Understanding Differentiable Volumetric Rendering*
- *Chapter 6, Exploring Neural Radiance Fields (NeRF)*

3

Fitting Deformable Mesh Models to Raw Point Clouds

In this chapter, we are going to discuss a project for using deformable mesh models for fitting raw point cloud observations potentially coming from a raw depth camera sensing result. Raw point cloud observations from depth cameras are usually in the format of point clouds without any information on how these points are connected; that is, the point clouds don't contain information about how surfaces can be formed from the points. This is contrary to a mesh, where the list of faces defined by the mesh shows us how the surfaces are. Such information on how points can be gathered into surfaces is important for downstream postprocessing, such as denoising and object detection. For example, if one point is isolated without any connection to any of the other points, then the point may likely be a false detection by the sensor.

Thus, reconstructing the surface information from point clouds is usually a standard step in 3D data processing pipelines. There exists a large body of prior-art literature on 3D surface reconstruction from points clouds, such as Poisson reconstruction. Using deformable mesh models for surface reconstruction is also among the frequently used methods. The method of fitting deformable mesh models for point clouds discussed in this chapter is a practical and simple baseline method.

The method presented in this chapter is based on PyTorch optimization. The method is another perfect demonstration of how optimization using PyTorch works. We will explain the optimization in reasonable detail, so that you can further improve your understanding of PyTorch optimization.

Loss functions are very important in most deep learning algorithms. Here, we will also discuss which loss functions we should use and the loss functions that have conventionally been contained in PyTorch3D. Luckily, many well-known loss functions have been implemented in many modern 3D deep learning frameworks and libraries, such as PyTorch3D. In this chapter, we are going to learn about many such loss functions.

In this chapter, we're going to cover the following main topics:

- Fitting meshes to point clouds – the problem
- Formulating the mesh model fitting problem as an optimization problem
- Loss functions for regularization
- Implementing the mesh fitting with PyTorch3D

Technical requirements

To run the example code snippets in this book, you should ideally have a computer that has a GPU. However, running the code snippets with only CPUs is not impossible.

The recommended computer configuration includes the following:

- A GPU, for example, the GTX series or RTX series, with at least 8 GB of memory
- Python 3
- The PyTorch and PyTorch3D libraries

The code snippets with this chapter can be found at `https://github.com/PacktPublishing/3D-Deep-Learning-with-Python`.

Fitting meshes to point clouds – the problem

Real-world depth cameras, such as LiDAR, time-of-flight cameras, and stereo vision cameras, usually output either depth images or point clouds. For example, in the case of time-of-flight cameras, a modulated light ray is projected from the camera to the world, and the depth at each pixel is measured from the phase of the reflected light rays received at the pixel. Thus, at each pixel, we can usually get one depth measurement and one reflected light amplitude measurement. However, other than the sampled depth information, we usually do not have direct measurements of the surfaces. For example, we cannot measure the smoothness or norm of the surface directly.

Similarly, in the case of stereo vision cameras, at each time slot, the camera can take two RGB images from the camera pair at roughly the same time. The camera then estimates the depth by finding the pixel correspondences between the two images. The output is thus a depth estimation at each pixel. Again, the camera cannot give us any direct measurements of surfaces.

However, in many real-world applications, surface information is sought. For example, in robotic picking tasks, usually, we need to find regions on an object such that the robotic hands can grasp firmly. In such a scenario, it is usually desirable that the regions are large in size and reasonably flat.

There are many other scenarios in which we want to fit a (deformable) mesh model to a point cloud. For example, there are some machine vision applications where we have the mesh model for an industrial part and the point cloud measurement from the depth camera has an unknown orientation and pose. In this case, finding a fitting of the mesh model to the point cloud would recover the unknown object pose.

For another example, in human face tracking, sometimes, we want to fit a deformable face mesh model to point cloud measurements, such that we can recover the identity of the human being and/or facial expressions.

Loss functions are central concepts in almost all optimizations. Essentially, to fit a point cloud, we need to design a loss function, such that when the loss function is minimized, the mesh as the optimization variable fits to the point cloud.

Actually, selecting the right loss function is usually a critical design decision in many real-world projects. Different choices of loss function usually result in significantly different system performance. The requirements for a loss function usually include at least the following properties:

- The loss function needs to have desirable numerical properties, such as smooth, convex, without the issue of vanishing gradients, and so on

- The loss function (and its gradients) can be easily computed; for example, they can be efficiently computed on GPUs

- The loss function is a good measurement of model fitting; that is, minimizing the loss function results in a satisfactory mesh model fitting for the input point clouds

Other than one primary loss function in such model fitting optimization problems, we usually also need to have other loss functions for regularizing the model fitting. For example, if we have some prior knowledge that the surfaces should be smooth, then we usually need to introduce an additional regularization loss function, such that not-smooth meshes would be penalized more.

An example of point cloud measurement using a pedestrian is shown in *Figure 3.1*. In the later sections of this chapter, we are going to discuss a deformable mesh-based approach for fitting a mesh model to point clouds. This point cloud is in the `pedestrian.ply` file, which can be downloaded from the book's GitHub page. The point cloud can be visualized by using the provided code snippet in `vis_input.py`.

Figure 3.1: An example of a 3D point cloud as the output of a depth
camera; note that the point density is relatively low

We have discussed the problem of fitting a mesh to a point cloud. Now, let us talk about how to formulate an optimization problem.

Formulating a deformable mesh fitting problem into an optimization problem

In this section, we are going to talk about how to formulate the mesh fitting problem into an optimization problem. One key observation here is that object surfaces such as pedestrians can always be continuously deformed into a sphere. Thus, the approach we are going to take will start from the surface of a sphere and deform the surface to minimize a cost function.

The cost function should be chosen such that it is a good measurement of how similar the point cloud is to the mesh. Here, we choose the major cost function to be the Chamfer set distance. The Chamfer distance is defined between two sets of points as follows:

$$CD(S_1, S_2) = \frac{1}{|S_1|} \sum_{x \in S_1} \min_{y \in S_2} \|x - y\|_2^2 + \frac{1}{|S_2|} \sum_{y \in S_2} \min_{y \in S_2} \|x - y\|_2^2$$

The Chamfer distance is symmetric and is a sum of two terms. In the first term, for each point x in the first point cloud, the closest point y in the other point cloud is found. For each such pair x and y, their distance is obtained and the distances for all the pairs are summed up. Similarly, in the second term, for each y in the second point cloud, one x is found and the distances between such x and y pairs are summed up.

Generally speaking, the Chamfer distance is the distance between two point clouds. If the two point clouds are identical, or very similar, then the Chamfer distance can be zero or very small. If the two point clouds are far away, then their Chamfer distance can be large.

In PyTorch3D, an implementation of Chamfer distance is provided in `pytorch3d.loss.chamfer_distance`. Not only the forward loss function calculation is provided, but we can also compute gradients for back-propagation easily using this implementation.

For fitting meshes to point clouds, we first randomly sample some points from a mesh model and then optimize the Chamfer distances between the sampled points from the mesh model and the input point cloud. The random sampling is achieved by `pytorch3d.ops.sample_points_from_meshes`. Again, we can compute the gradients for back-propagation from `pytorch3d.ops.sample_points_from_meshes`.

Now, we have a basic version of the optimization problem. However, we may still need some loss functions for the regularization of this problem. We will dive into these issues in the next section.

Loss functions for regularization

In the previous section, we successfully formulated the deformable mesh fitting problem into an optimization problem. However, the approach of directly optimizing this primary loss function can be problematic. The issues lie in that there may exist multiple mesh models that can be good fits to the same point cloud. These mesh models that are good fits may include some mesh models that are far away from smooth meshes.

On the other hand, we usually have prior knowledge about pedestrians. For example, the surfaces of pedestrians are usually smooth, the surface norms are smooth also. Thus, even if a non-smooth mesh is close to the input point cloud in terms of Chamfer distance, we know with a certain level of confidence that it is far away from the ground truth.

Machine learning literature has provided solutions for excluding such undesirable non-smooth solutions for several decades. The solution is called **regularization**. Essentially, the loss we want to optimize is chosen to be a sum of multiple loss functions. Certainly, the first term of the sum will be the primary Chamfer distance. The other terms are for penalizing surface non-smoothness and norm non-smoothness.

In the next several subsections, we are going to discuss several such loss functions, including the following:

- Mesh Laplacian smoothing loss
- Mesh normal consistency loss
- Mesh edge loss

Mesh Laplacian smoothing loss

The mesh Laplacian is a discrete version of the well-known Laplace-Beltrami operator. One version (usually called uniform Laplacian) is as follows:

$$\delta_i = \sum_{i,j \ are \ edges} v_i - v_j$$

In the preceding definition, the Laplacian at the i-th vertex is just a sum of differences, where each difference is between the coordinates of the current vertex and those of a neighboring vertex.

The Laplacian is a measurement for smoothness. If the i-th vertex and its neighbors lie all within one plane, then the Laplacian should be zero. Here, we are using a uniform version of the Laplacian, where the contribution to the sum from each neighbor is equally weighted. There are more complicated versions of Laplacians, where the preceding contributions are weighted according to various schemes.

Essentially, including this loss function in the optimization would result in smoother solutions. One implementation for the mesh Laplacian smoothing loss (including multiple other versions than the uniform one) can be found at `pytorch3d.loss.mesh_laplacian_smoothing`. Again, gradient computations for back-propagation are enabled.

Mesh normal consistency loss

The mesh normal consistency loss is a loss function for penalizing the distances between adjacent normal vectors on the mesh. One implementation can be found at `pytorch3d.loss.mesh_normal_consistency`.

Mesh edge loss

Mesh edge loss is for penalizing long edges in meshes. For example, in the mesh model fitting problem we consider in this chapter, we want to eventually obtain a solution, such that the obtained mesh model fits the input point cloud uniformly. In other words, each local region of the point cloud is covered by small triangles of the mesh. Otherwise, the mesh model cannot capture the fine details of slowly varying surfaces, meaning the model may not be that accurate or trustworthy.

The aforementioned problem can be easily avoided by including the mesh edge loss in the objective function. The mesh edge loss is essentially a sum of all the edge lengths in the mesh. One implementation of the mesh edge loss can be found at `pytorch3d.loss.mesh_edge_loss`.

Now, we have covered all the concepts and mathematics for this mesh fitting problem. Next, let us dive into how the problem can be coded by using Python and PyTorch3D.

Implementing the mesh fitting with PyTorch3D

The input point cloud is contained in `pedestrian.ply`. The mesh can be visualized using the `vis_input.py` code snippet. The main code snippet for fitting a mesh model to the point cloud is contained in `deform1.py`:

1. We will start by importing the needed packages:

```
import os
import sys
import torch
from pytorch3d.io import load_ply, save_ply
from pytorch3d.io import load_obj, save_obj
from pytorch3d.structures import Meshes
from pytorch3d.utils import ico_sphere
from pytorch3d.ops import sample_points_from_meshes
from pytorch3d.loss import (
    chamfer_distance,
    mesh_edge_loss,
    mesh_laplacian_smoothing,
    mesh_normal_consistency,
)
import numpy as np
```

2.   We then declare a PyTorch device. If you have GPUs, then the device would be created to use GPUs. Otherwise, the device has to use CPUs:

```
if torch.cuda.is_available():
    device = torch.device("cuda:0")
else:
    device = torch.device("cpu")
    print("WARNING: CPU only, this will be slow!")
```

3.   We will load the point cloud from `pedestrian.ply`. Now, `load_ply` is a PyTorch3D function that loads the .ply file and outputs `verts` and `faces`. In this case, `verts` is a PyTorch tensor. `faces` is an empty PyTorch tensor because `pedestrian.ply` actually does not contain any faces. The `to` member function moves the tensors to the device; if the device uses GPUs, then `verts` and `faces` are transmitted to the GPU memories:

```
verts, faces = load_ply("pedestrian.ply")
verts = verts.to(device)
faces = faces.to(device)
```

4.   We then run some normalization and change the tensor shapes for later processing:

```
center = verts.mean(0)
verts = verts - center
scale = max(verts.abs().max(0)[0])
verts = verts / scale
verts = verts[None, :, :]
```

5.   In the next step, we create a mesh variable called `src_mesh` by using the `ico_sphere` PyTorch3D function. The `ico_sphere` function essentially creates a mesh representing roughly a sphere. This `src_mesh` will be our optimization variable; it will start as a sphere and then be optimized to fit the point cloud:

```
src_mesh = ico_sphere(4, device)
```

6.   In the next step, we want to define a `deform_verts` variable. `deform_verts` is a tensor of vertex displacements, where for each vertex in `src_mesh`, there is a vertex displacement of the three-dimensional vector. We are going to optimize `deform_verts` for finding the optimal deformable mesh:

```
src_vert = src_mesh.verts_list()
deform_verts = torch.full(src_vert[0].shape, 0.0,
device=device, requires_grad=True)
```

7. We define an SGD optimizer with `deform_verts` as the optimization variable:

```
optimizer = torch.optim.SGD([deform_verts], lr=1.0,
momentum=0.9)
```

8. We define a batch of weights for different loss functions. As we have mentioned, we need multiple loss functions, including the primary one and the regularization loss functions. The final loss will be a weighted sum of the different loss functions. Here is where we define the weights:

```
w_chamfer = 1.0
w_edge = 1.0
w_normal = 0.01
w_laplacian = 0.1
```

9. We are then ready for going into the major optimization iterations. We are going to iterate 2,000 times for computing the loss function, computing the gradients, and going along the gradient descent directions. Each iteration starts with `optimizer.zero_grad()`, which will reset all the gradients, the `loss` variable is then computed, and the gradient back-propagation is then computed in `loss.backward()`; the going along the gradient descent direction is done in `optimizer.step()`.

    For us to be able to compute the Chamfer distance, during each iteration, we randomly sample some points from the deformed mesh model by using a PyTorch3D function called `sample_points_from_meshes`. Note that the `sample_points_from_meshes` function supports gradient back-propagation computations.

    We also use three other loss functions for regularization, `mesh_edge_loss`, `mesh_normal_consistency`, and `mesh_laplacian_smooth`. The final `loss` variable is actually the weighted sum of the four loss functions:

```
for i in range(0, 2000):
    print("i = ", i)
    optimizer.zero_grad()
    new_src_mesh = src_mesh.offset_verts(deform_verts)
    sample_trg = verts
    sample_src = sample_points_from_meshes(new_src_mesh,
verts.shape[1])
    loss_chamfer, _ = chamfer_distance(sample_trg,
sample_src)
    loss_edge = mesh_edge_loss(new_src_mesh)
    loss_normal = mesh_normal_consistency(new_src_mesh)
    loss_laplacian = mesh_laplacian_smoothing(new_src_
mesh, method="uniform")
```

```
loss = (
    loss_chamfer * w_chamfer
    + loss_edge * w_edge
    + loss_normal * w_normal
    + loss_laplacian * w_laplacian
)
loss.backward()
optimizer.step()
```

10. We then extract the obtained vertices and faces from the `new_src_mesh` variable and then resume its original center location and scale:

```
final_verts, final_faces = new_src_mesh.get_mesh_verts_
faces(0)
final_verts = final_verts * scale + center
```

11. Finally, the obtained mesh model is saved in the `deform1.ply` file:

```
final_obj = os.path.join("./", "deform1.ply")
save_ply(final_obj, final_verts, final_faces, ascii=True)
```

Figure 3.2: Optimized deformed mesh model. Note that we have
far more points than the original input point cloud

The obtained mesh can be visualized on your screen by using vis1.py. One screenshot of the obtained mesh is shown in *Figure 3.2*. Note that compared to the original input point cloud, the optimized mesh model actually contains far more points (2,500 compared with 239). The obtained surfaces seem to be smoother than the original input points also.

The experiment of not using any regularization loss functions

What if we don't use any of these regularization loss functions? We run an experiment using the code in deform2.py. The only difference between the code snippet in deform2.py and the one in deform1.py is the following lines:

```
w_chamfer = 1.0
w_edge = 0.0
w_normal = 0.00
w_laplacian = 0.0
```

Note that all the weights have been set to zero, except the one for the Chamfer loss function. Essentially, we are not using any loss functions for regularization. The resulting mesh can be visualized on your screen by running vis2.py. A screenshot is shown in *Figure 3.3*:

Figure 3.3: Mesh obtained without using any loss functions for regularization

Note that the obtained mesh in *Figure 3.3* is not smooth and is unlikely to be close to the actual ground-truth surfaces.

The experiment of using only the mesh edge loss

This time, we are going to use the following set of weights. The code snippet is in `deform3.py`:

```
w_chamfer = 1.0
w_edge = 1.0
w_normal = 0.00
w_laplacian = 0.0
```

The obtained mesh model is in `deform3.ply`. The mesh can be visualized on your screen by using `vis3.py`. A screenshot of the mesh is shown in *Figure 3.4*:

Figure 3.4: Obtained mesh using only the mesh_edge_loss regularization

From *Figure 3.4*, we can observe that the obtained mesh is much smoother than the one in *Figure 3.3*. However, it seems that there are some rapid changes in the surface normal. Actually, you can try out other weights on your own to see how these loss functions affect the final outcomes.

Summary

In this chapter, we talked about an approach to fitting deformable mesh models to a point cloud. As we have discussed, obtaining meshes from point clouds is usually a standard step in many 3D computer vision pipelines. The fitting approach in this chapter can be used as a simple baseline approach in practice.

From this deformable mesh fitting approach, we learned how to use PyTorch optimization. We also learned about many loss functions and their PyTorch3D implementations, including Chamfer distances, mesh edge loss, mesh Laplacian smoothing loss, and mesh normal consistency loss.

We learned when these loss functions should be used and for what purposes. We saw several experiments for showing how the loss functions affect the final outcome. You are also encouraged to run your own experiments with different combinations of loss functions and weights.

In the next chapter, we will discuss a very exciting 3D deep learning technique called differentiable rendering. Actually, we will have several differentiable-rendering-related chapters in this book. The next chapter will be the first one of these chapters.

4

Learning Object Pose Detection and Tracking by Differentiable Rendering

In this chapter, we are going to explore an object pose detection and tracking project by using differentiable rendering. In object pose detection, we are interested in detecting the orientation and location of a certain object. For example, we may be given the camera model and object mesh model and need to estimate the object orientation and position from one image of the object. In the approach in this chapter, we are going to formulate such a pose estimation problem as an optimization problem, where the object pose is fitted to the image observation.

The same approach as the aforementioned can also be used for object pose tracking, where we have already estimated the object pose in the 1, 2,…, up to t-1 time slots and want to estimate the object pose at the t time slot, based on one image observation of the object at t time.

One important technique we will use in this chapter is called differentiable rendering, a super-exciting topic currently explored in deep learning. For example, the CVPR 2021 Best Paper Award winner *GIRAFFE: representing scenes as compositional generative neural feature fields* uses differentiable rendering as one important component in its pipeline.

Rendering is the process of projecting 3D physical models (a mesh model for the object, or a camera model) into 2D images. It is an imitation of the physical process of image formation. Many 3D computer vision tasks can be considered as an inverse of the rendering process – that is, in many computer vision problems, we want to start from 2D images to estimate the 3D physical models (meshes, point cloud segmentation, object poses, or camera positions).

Thus, a very natural idea that has been discussed in the computer vision community for several decades is that we can formulate many 3D computer vision problems as optimization problems, where the optimization variables are the 3D models (meshes, or point cloud voxels), and the objective functions are certain similarity measures between the rendered images and the observed images.

To efficiently solve such an optimization problem as the aforementioned, the rendering process should be differentiable. For example, if the rendering is differentiable, we can use the end-to-end approach to train a deep learning model to solve the problem. However, as will be discussed in more detail in the latter sections, conventional rendering processes are not differentiable. Thus, we need to modify the conventional approaches to make them differentiable. We will discuss how we can do that at great length in the following section.

Thus, in this chapter, we will cover first the *why differentiable rendering* problem and then the *how differentiable problems* problem. We will then talk about what 3D computer vision problems can usually be solved by using differentiable rendering. We will dedicate a significant part of the chapter to a concrete example of using differentiable rendering to solve object pose estimation. We will present coding examples in the process.

In this chapter, we're going to cover the following main topics:

- Why differentiable renderings are needed

- How to make rendering differentiable

- What problems can be solved by differentiable rendering

- The object pose estimation problem

Technical requirements

In order to run the example code snippets in this book, you need to have a computer ideally with a GPU. However, running the code snippets with only CPUs is not impossible.

The recommended computer configuration includes the following:

- A GPU such as the GTX series or RTX series with at least 8 GB of memory

- Python 3

- The PyTorch and PyTorch3D libraries

The code snippets with this chapter can be found at `https://github.com/PacktPublishing/3D-Deep-Learning-with-Python`.

Why we want to have differentiable rendering

The physical process of image formation is a mapping from 3D models to 2D images. As shown in the example in *Figure 4.1*, depending on the positions of the red and blue spheres in 3D (two possible configurations are shown on the left-hand side), we may get different 2D images (the images corresponding to the two configurations are shown on the right-hand side).

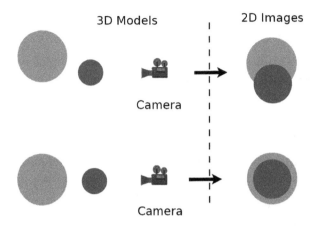

Figure 4.1: The image formation process is a mapping from the 3D models to 2D images

Many 3D computer vision problems are a reversal of image formation. In these problems, we are usually given 2D images and need to estimate the 3D models from the 2D images. For example, in *Figure 4.2*, we are given the 2D image shown on the right-hand side and the question is, *which 3D model is the one that corresponds to the observed image?*

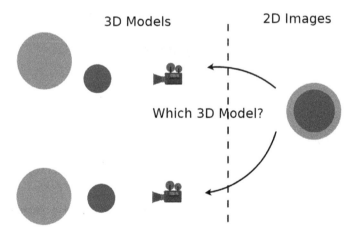

Figure 4.2: Many 3D computer vision problems are based on 2D images given to estimate 3D models

According to some ideas that were first discussed in the computer vision community decades ago, we can formulate the problem as an optimization problem. In this case, the optimization variables here are the position of two 3D spheres. We want to optimize the two centers, such that the rendered images are like the preceding 2D observed image. To measure similarity precisely, we need to use a cost function – for example, we can use pixel-wise mean-square errors. We then need to compute a gradient from the cost function to the two centers of spheres, so that we can minimize the cost function iteratively by going toward the gradient descent direction.

However, we can calculate a gradient from the cost function to the optimization variables only under the condition that the mapping from the optimization variables to the cost functions is differentiable, which implies that the rendering process is also differentiable.

How to make rendering differentiable

In this section, we are going to discuss why the conventional rendering algorithms are not differentiable. We will discuss the approach used in PyTorch3D, which makes the rendering differentiable.

Rendering is an imitation of the physical process of image formation. This physical process of image formation itself is differentiable in many cases. Suppose that the surface is normal and the material properties of the object are all smooth. Then, the pixel color in the example is a differentiable function of the positions of the spheres.

However, there are cases where the pixel color is not a smooth function of the position. This can happen at the occlusion boundaries, for example. This is shown in *Figure 4.3*, where the blue sphere is at a location that would occlude the red sphere at that view if the blue sphere moved up a little bit. The pixel moved at that view is thus not a differentiable function of the sphere center locations.

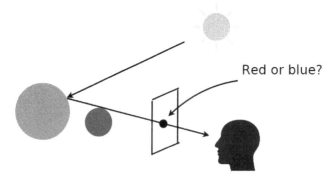

Figure 4.3: The image formation is not a smooth function at occlusion boundaries

When we use conventional rendering algorithms, information about local gradients is lost due to discretization. As we discussed in the previous chapters, rasterization is a step of rendering where for each pixel on the imaging plane, we find the most relevant mesh face (or decide that no relevant mesh face can be found).

In conventional rasterization, for each pixel, we generate a ray from the camera center going through the pixel on the imaging plane. We will find all the mesh faces that intersect with this ray. In the conventional approach, the rasterizer will only return the mesh face that is nearest to the camera. The returned mesh face will then be passed to the shader, which is the next step of the rendering pipeline. The shader will then be applied to one of the shading algorithms (such as the Lambertian model or Phong model) to determine the pixel color. This step of choosing the mesh to render is a non-differentiable process, since it is mathematically modeled as a step function.

There has been a large body of literature in the computer vision community on how to make rendering differentiable. The differentiable rendering implemented in the PyTorch3D library mainly used the approach in *Soft Rasterizer* by Liu, Li, Chen, and Li (arXiv:1904.01786).

The main idea of differentiable rendering is illustrated in *Figure 4.4*. In the rasterization step, instead of returning only one relevant mesh face, we will find all the mesh faces, such that the distance of the mesh face to the ray is within a certain threshold. In PyTorch3D, this threshold can be set at `RasterizationSettings.blur_radius`. We can also control the maximal number of faces to be returned by setting `RasterizationSettings.faces_per_pixel`.

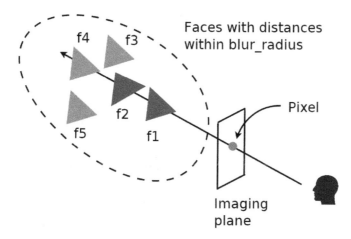

Figure 4.4: Differentiable rendering by weighted averaging of all the relevant mesh faces

Next, the renderer needs to calculate a probability map for each mesh face as follows, where `dist` represents the distance between the mesh face and the ray, and sigma is a hyperparameter. In Pytorch3D, the `sigma` parameter can be set at `BlendParams.sigma`. Simply put, this probability map is a probability that this mesh face covers this image pixel. The distance can be negative if the ray intersects the mesh face.

$$D_j = sigmoid(\frac{-dist_j}{\sigma})$$

Next, the pixel color is determined by the weighted averages of the shading results of all the mesh faces returned by the rasterizer. The weight for each mesh face depends on its inverse depth value, z, and probability map, D, as shown in the following equation. Because this z value is the inverse depth, any mesh faces closer to the camera have larger z values than the mesh faces far away from the camera. The weight, w_b, is a small weight for the background color. The parameter gamma here is a hyperparameter. In PyTorch3D, this parameter can be set to `BlendParams.gamma`:

$$w_j = D_j \exp\left(\frac{z_j}{\gamma}\right), w_b = \exp\left(\frac{\epsilon}{\gamma}\right)$$

Thus, the final pixel color can be determined by the following equation:

$$I = \frac{(\sum_j w_j c_j) + w_b c_b}{(\sum_j w_j) + w_b}$$

The PyTorch3D implementation of differential rendering also computes an alpha value for each image pixel. This alpha value represents how likely the image pixel is in the foreground, the ray intersects at least one mesh face, as shown in *Figure 4.4*. We want to compute this alpha value and make it differentiable. In a soft rasterizer, the alpha value is computed from the probability maps, as follows.

$$\alpha = 1 - \prod_j (1 - D_j)$$

Now that we have learned how to make rendering differentiable, we will see how to use it for various purposes.

What problems can be solved by using differentiable rendering

As mentioned earlier, differentiable rendering has been discussed in the computer vision community for decades. In the past, differentiable rendering was used for single-view mesh reconstruction, image-based shape fitting, and more. In the following sections of this chapter, we are going to show a concrete example of using differentiable rendering for rigid object pose estimation and tracking.

Differentiable rendering is a technique in that we can formulate the estimation problems in 3D computer vision into optimization problems. It can be applied to a wide range of problems. More interestingly, one exciting recent trend is to combine differentiable rendering with deep learning. Usually, differentiable rendering is used as the generator part of the deep learning models. The whole pipeline can thus be trained end to end.

The object pose estimation problem

In this section, we are going to show a concrete example of using differentiable rendering for 3D computer vision problems. The problem is object pose estimation from one single observed image. In addition, we assume that we have the 3D mesh model of the object.

For example, we assume we have the 3D mesh model for a toy cow and teapot, as shown in *Figure 4.5* and *Figure 4.7* respectively. Now, suppose we have taken one image of the toy cow and teapot. Thus, we have one RGB image of the toy cow, as shown in *Figure 4.6*, and one silhouette image of the teapot, as shown in *Figure 4.8*. The problem is then to estimate the orientation and location of the toy cow and teapot at the moments when these images are taken.

Because it is cumbersome to rotate and move the meshes, we choose instead to fix the orientations and locations of the meshes and optimize the orientations and locations of the cameras. By assuming that the camera orientations are always pointing toward the meshes, we can further simplify the problem, such that all we need to optimize is the camera locations.

Thus, we formulate our optimization problem, such that the optimization variables will be the camera locations. By using differentiable rendering, we can render RGB images and silhouette images for the two meshes. The rendered images are compared with the observed images and, thus, loss functions between the rendered images and observed images can be calculated. Here, we use mean-square errors as the loss function. Because everything is differentiable, we can then compute gradients from the loss functions to the optimization variables. Gradient descent algorithms can then be used to find the best camera positions, such that the rendered images are matched to the observed images.

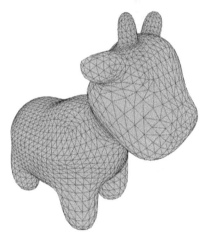

Figure 4.5: Mesh model for a toy cow

The following image shows the RGB output for the cow:

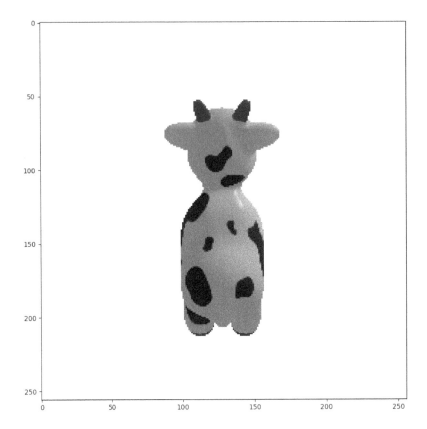

Figure 4.6: Observed RGB image for the toy cow

The following figure shows the mesh for a teapot:

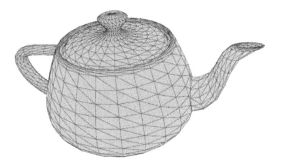

Figure 4.7: Mesh model for a teapot

The following figure shows the silhouette of the teapot:

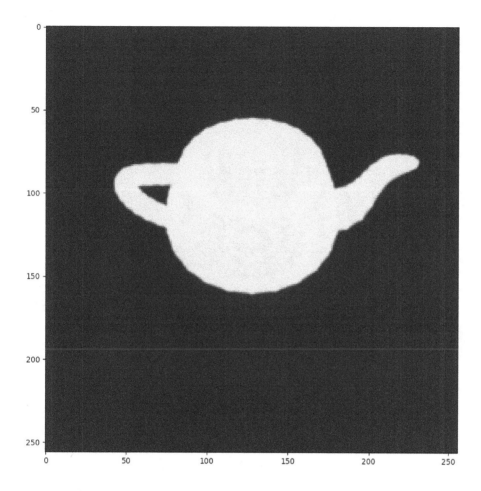

Figure 4.8: Observed silhouette of the teapot

Now that we know the problem and how to work on it, let's start coding in the next section.

How it is coded

The code is provided in the repository in the chap4 folder as diff_render.py. The mesh model of the teapot is provided in the data subfolder as teapot.obj. We will run through the code as follows:

1. The code in diff_render.py starts by importing the needed packages:

```
import os
import torch
import numpy as np
import torch.nn as nn
import matplotlib.pyplot as plt
from skimage import img_as_ubyte

from pytorch3d.io import load_obj
from pytorch3d.structures import Meshes

from pytorch3d.renderer import (
FoVPerspectiveCameras, look_at_view_transform, look_at_
rotation,
RasterizationSettings, MeshRenderer, MeshRasterizer,
BlendParams,
SoftSilhouetteShader, HardPhongShader, PointLights,
TexturesVertex,
)
```

2. In the next step, we declare a PyTorch device. If you have GPUs, then the device will be created to use GPUs. Otherwise, the device has to use CPUs:

```
if torch.cuda.is_available():
    device = torch.device("cuda:0")
else:
    device = torch.device("cpu")
    print("WARNING: CPU only, this will be slow!")
```

3. We then define output_dir in the following line. When we run the codes in diff_render. py, the codes will generate some rendered images for each optimization iteration, so that we can see how the optimization works step by step. All the generated rendered images by the code will be put in this output_dir folder.

```
output_dir = './result_teapot'
```

4. We then load the mesh model from the `./data/teapot.obj` file. Because this mesh model does not come with textures (material colors), we create an all-one tensor and make the tensor the texture for the mesh model. Eventually, we obtain a mesh model with textures as the `teapot_mesh` variable:

```
verts, faces_idx, _ = load_obj("./data/teapot.obj")
faces = faces_idx.verts_idx

verts_rgb = torch.ones_like(verts)[None]   # (1, V, 3)
textures = TexturesVertex(verts_features=verts_rgb.
to(device))

teapot_mesh = Meshes(
    verts=[verts.to(device)],
    faces=[faces.to(device)],
    textures=textures
)
```

5. Next, we define a camera model in the following line.

```
cameras = FoVPerspectiveCameras(device=device)
```

6. In the next step, we are going to define a differentiable renderer called `silhouette_renderer`. Each renderer has mainly two components, such as one rasterizer for finding relevant mesh faces for each image pixel, one shader for determining the image pixel colors, and so on. In this example, we actually use a soft silhouette shader, which outputs an alpha value for each image pixel. The alpha value is a real number ranging from 0 to 1, which indicates whether this image pixel is a part of the foreground or background. Note that the hyperparameters for the shader are defined in the `blend_params` variables, the `sigma` parameter is for computing the probability maps, and gamma is for computing weights for mesh faces.

    Here, we use `MeshRasterizer` for rasterization. Note that the parameter `blur_radius` is the threshold for finding relevant mesh faces and `faces_per_pixel` is the maximum number of mesh faces that will be returned for each image pixel:

```
blend_params = BlendParams(sigma=1e-4, gamma=1e-4)

raster_settings = RasterizationSettings(
    image_size=256,
    blur_radius=np.log(1. / 1e-4 - 1.) * blend_params.
```

```
    sigma,
        faces_per_pixel=100,
    )


    silhouette_renderer = MeshRenderer(
        rasterizer=MeshRasterizer(
            cameras=cameras,
            raster_settings=raster_settings
        ),
        shader=SoftSilhouetteShader(blend_params=blend_
    params)
    )
```

7. We then define phong_renderer as follows. This phong_renderer is mainly used for visualization of the optimization process. Basically, at each optimization iteration, we will render one RGB image according to the camera position at that iteration. Note that this renderer is only used for visualization purposes, thus it is not a differentiable renderer. You can actually tell that phong_renderer is not a differentiable one by noticing the following:

    *   It uses HardPhoneShader, which takes only one mesh face as input for each image pixel

    *   It uses MeshRenderer with a blur_radius value of 0.0 and faces_per_pixel is set to 1

8. A light source, lights, is then defined with a location of 2.0, 2.0, and -2.0:

```
    raster_settings = RasterizationSettings(
        image_size=256,
        blur_radius=0.0,
        faces_per_pixel=1,
    )


    lights = PointLights(device=device, location=((2.0, 2.0,
    -2.0),))
    phong_renderer = MeshRenderer(
        rasterizer=MeshRasterizer(
            cameras=cameras,
            raster_settings=raster_settings
        ),
```

```
    shader=HardPhongShader(device=device,
cameras=cameras, lights=lights)
)
```

9. Next, we define a camera location and compute the corresponding rotation, R, and displacement, T, of the camera. This rotation and displacement are the target camera position – that is, we are going to generate an image from this camera position and use the image as the observed image in our problem:

```
distance = 3
elevation = 50.0
azimuth = 0.0


R, T = look_at_view_transform(distance, elevation,
azimuth, device=device)
```

10. Now, we generate an image, image_ref, from this camera position. The image_ref function has four channels, **RGBA** – **R** for red, **G** for green, **B** for blue, and **A** for alpha values. The image_ref function is also saved as target_rgb.png for our latter inspection:

```
silhouette = silhouette_renderer(meshes_world=teapot_
mesh, R=R, T=T)
image_ref = phong_renderer(meshes_world=teapot_mesh, R=R,
T=T)

silhouette = silhouette.cpu().numpy()
image_ref = image_ref.cpu().numpy()

plt.figure(figsize=(10, 10))
plt.imshow(silhouette.squeeze()[..., 3])   # only plot the
alpha channel of the RGBA image
plt.grid(False)
plt.savefig(os.path.join(output_dir, 'target_silhouette.
png'))
plt.close()


plt.figure(figsize=(10, 10))
plt.imshow(image_ref.squeeze())
```

```
plt.grid(False)
plt.savefig(os.path.join(output_dir, 'target_rgb.png'))
plt.close()
```

11. In the next step, we are going to define a `Model` class. This `Model` class is derived from `torch.nn.Module`; thus, as with many other PyTorch models, automatic gradient computations can be enabled for `Model`.

   `Model` has an initialization function, `__init__`, which takes the `meshes` input for mesh models, `renderer` for the renderer, and `image_ref` as the target image that the instance of `Model` will try to fit. The `__init__` function creates an `image_ref` buffer by using the `torch.nn.Module.register_buffer` function. Just a reminder for those who are not so familiar with this part of PyTorch – a buffer is something that can be saved as a part of `state_dict` and moved to different devices in `cuda()` and `cpu()`, with the rest of the model's parameters. However, the buffer is not updated by the optimizer.

   The `__init__` function also creates a model parameter, `camera_position`. As a model parameter, the `camera_position` variable can be updated by the optimizer. Note that the optimization variables now become the model parameters.

   The `Model` class also has a `forward` member function, which can do the forward computation and backward gradient propagation. The forward function renders a silhouette image from the current camera position and computes a loss function between the rendered image with `image_refer` – the observed image:

```
class Model(nn.Module):
    def __init__(self, meshes, renderer, image_ref):
        super().__init__()
        self.meshes = meshes
        self.device = meshes.device
        self.renderer = renderer

        image_ref = torch.from_numpy((image_ref[..., :3].
max(-1) != 1).astype(np.float32))
        self.register_buffer('image_ref', image_ref)

        self.camera_position = nn.Parameter(
            torch.from_numpy(np.array([3.0, 6.9, +2.5],
```

```
dtype=np.float32)).to(meshes.device))


    def forward(self):
        R = look_at_rotation(self.camera_position[None,
:], device=self.device)  # (1, 3, 3)
        T = -torch.bmm(R.transpose(1, 2), self.camera_
position[None, :, None])[:, :, 0]  # (1, 3)


        image = self.renderer(meshes_world=self.meshes.
clone(), R=R, T=T)
        loss = torch.sum((image[..., 3] - self.image_ref)
** 2)
        return loss, image
```

12. Now, we have already defined the Model class. We can then create an instance of the class and define an optimizer. Before running any optimization, we want to render an image to show the starting camera position. This silhouette image for the starting camera position will be saved to starting_silhouette.png:

```
model = Model(meshes=teapot_mesh, renderer=silhouette_
renderer, image_ref=image_ref).to(device)
optimizer = torch.optim.Adam(model.parameters(), lr=0.05)

_, image_init = model()
plt.figure(figsize=(10, 10))
plt.imshow(image_init.detach().squeeze().cpu().numpy()
[..., 3])
plt.grid(False)
plt.title("Starting Silhouette")
plt.savefig(os.path.join(output_dir, 'starting_
silhouette.png'))
plt.close()
```

13. Finally, we can run optimization iterations. During each optimization iteration, we will save the rendered image from the camera position to a file under the output_dir folder:

```
for i in range(0, 200):
    if i%10 == 0:
```

```
        print('i = ', i)
    optimizer.zero_grad()
    loss, _ = model()
    loss.backward()
    optimizer.step()

    if loss.item() < 500:
        break


    R = look_at_rotation(model.camera_position[None, :],
device=model.device)
    T = -torch.bmm(R.transpose(1, 2), model.camera_
position[None, :, None])[:, :, 0]  # (1, 3)
    image = phong_renderer(meshes_world=model.meshes.
clone(), R=R, T=T)
    image = image[0, ..., :3].detach().squeeze().cpu().
numpy()
    image = img_as_ubyte(image)

    plt.figure()
    plt.imshow(image[..., :3])
    plt.title("iter: %d, loss: %0.2f" % (i, loss.data))
    plt.axis("off")
    plt.savefig(os.path.join(output_dir, 'fitting_' +
str(i) + '.png'))
    plt.close()
```

Figure 4.9 shows the observed silhouette of the object (in this case, a teapot):

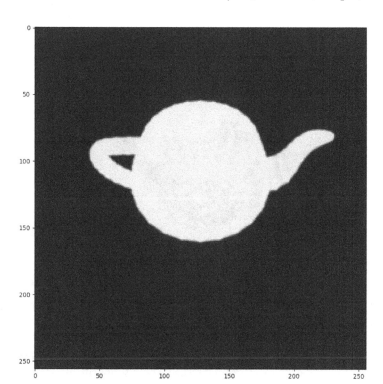

Figure 4.9: The silhouette of the teapot

We formulate the fitting problem as an optimization problem. The initial teapot position is illustrated in *Figure 4.10*.

iter: 0, loss: 8414.53

Figure 4.10: The initial position of the teapot

The final optimized teapot position is illustrated in *Figure 4.11*.

iter: 87, loss: 372.46

Figure 4.11: The final position of the teapot

An example of object pose estimation for both silhouette fitting and texture fitting

In the previous example, we estimated the object pose by silhouette fitting. In this section, we will present another example of object pose estimation by using both silhouette fitting and texture fitting. In 3D computer vision, we usually use texture to denote colors. Thus, in this example, we will use differentiable rendering to render RGB images according to the camera positions and optimize the camera position. The code is in `diff_render_texture.py`:

1. In this first step, we will import all the required packages:

    ```
    import os
    import torch
    import numpy as np
    import torch.nn as nn
    import matplotlib.pyplot as plt
    from skimage import img_as_ubyte

    from pytorch3d.io import load_objs_as_meshes

    from pytorch3d.renderer import (
    FoVPerspectiveCameras, look_at_view_transform, look_at_
    rotation,
    ```

```
RasterizationSettings, MeshRenderer, MeshRasterizer,
BlendParams,
SoftSilhouetteShader, HardPhongShader, PointLights,
SoftPhongShader
)
```

2. Next, we create the PyTorch device using either GPUs or CPUs:

```
if torch.cuda.is_available():
    device = torch.device("cuda:0")
    torch.cuda.set_device(device)
else:
    device = torch.device("cpu")
```

3. We set `output_dir` as `result_cow`. This will be the folder where we save the fitting results:

```
output_dir = './result_cow'
```

4. We load the mesh model of a toy cow from the `cow.obj` file:

```
obj_filename = "./data/cow_mesh/cow.obj"
cow_mesh = load_objs_as_meshes([obj_filename],
device=device)
```

5. We define cameras and light sources as follows:

```
cameras = FoVPerspectiveCameras(device=device)
lights = PointLights(device=device, location=((2.0, 2.0,
-2.0),))
```

6. Next, we create a `renderer_silhouette` renderer. This is the differentiable renderer for rendering silhouette images. Note the `blur_radius` and `faces_per_pixel` numbers. This renderer is mainly used in silhouette fitting:

```
blend_params = BlendParams(sigma=1e-4, gamma=1e-4)
raster_settings = RasterizationSettings(
    image_size=256,
    blur_radius=np.log(1. / 1e-4 - 1.) * blend_params.
sigma,
    faces_per_pixel=100,
)
```

```
renderer_silhouette = MeshRenderer(
    rasterizer=MeshRasterizer(
        cameras=cameras,
        raster_settings=raster_settings
    ),
    shader=SoftSilhouetteShader(blend_params=blend_
params)
)
```

7. Next, we create a `renderer_textured` renderer. This renderer is another differentiable renderer, mainly used for rendering RGB images:

```
sigma = 1e-4
raster_settings_soft = RasterizationSettings(
    image_size=256,
    blur_radius=np.log(1. / 1e-4 - 1.)*sigma,
    faces_per_pixel=50,
)
renderer_textured = MeshRenderer(
    rasterizer=MeshRasterizer(
        cameras=cameras,
        raster_settings=raster_settings_soft
    ),
    shader=SoftPhongShader(device=device,
        cameras=cameras,
        lights=lights)
)
```

8. Next, we create a `phong_renderer` renderer. This renderer is mainly used for visualization. The preceding differentiable renders tend to create blurry images. Therefore, it would be nice for us to have a renderer that can create sharp images:

```
raster_settings = RasterizationSettings(
    image_size=256,
    blur_radius=0.0,
    faces_per_pixel=1,
)
phong_renderer = MeshRenderer(
    rasterizer=MeshRasterizer(
```

```
        cameras=cameras,
        raster_settings=raster_settings
    ),
    shader=HardPhongShader(device=device,
cameras=cameras, lights=lights)
)
```

9. Next, we will define a camera position and the corresponding camera rotation and position. This will be the camera position where the observed image is taken. As in the previous example, we optimize the camera orientation and position instead of the object orientation and position. Also, we assume that the camera is always pointing toward the object. Thus, we only need to optimize the camera position:

```
distance = 3
elevation = 50.0
azimuth = 0.0
R, T = look_at_view_transform(distance, elevation,
azimuth, device=device)
```

10. Next, we create the observed images and save them to target_silhouette.png and target_rgb.png. The images are also stored in the silhouette and image_ref variables:

```
silhouette = renderer_silhouette(meshes_world=cow_mesh,
R=R, T=T)
image_ref = phong_renderer(meshes_world=cow_mesh, R=R,
T=T)
silhouette = silhouette.cpu().numpy()
image_ref = image_ref.cpu().numpy()

plt.figure(figsize=(10, 10))
plt.imshow(silhouette.squeeze()[..., 3])
plt.grid(False)
plt.savefig(os.path.join(output_dir, 'target_silhouette.
png'))
plt.close()

plt.figure(figsize=(10, 10))
plt.imshow(image_ref.squeeze())
plt.grid(False)
plt.savefig(os.path.join(output_dir, 'target_rgb.png'))
```

```
plt.close()
```

11. We modify the definition for the `Model` class as follows. The most notable changes from the previous example are that now we will render both the alpha channel image and the RGB images and compare them with the observed images. The mean-square losses at the alpha channel and RGB channels are weighted to give the final loss value:

```python
class Model(nn.Module):
    def __init__(self, meshes, renderer_silhouette,
renderer_textured, image_ref, weight_silhouette, weight_
texture):
        super().__init__()
        self.meshes = meshes
        self.device = meshes.device
        self.renderer_silhouette = renderer_silhouette
        self.renderer_textured = renderer_textured

        self.weight_silhouette = weight_silhouette
        self.weight_texture = weight_texture

        image_ref_silhouette = torch.from_numpy((image_
ref[..., :3].max(-1) != 1).astype(np.float32))
        self.register_buffer('image_ref_silhouette',
image_ref_silhouette)

        image_ref_textured = torch.from_numpy((image_
ref[..., :3]).astype(np.float32))
        self.register_buffer('image_ref_textured', image_
ref_textured)

        self.camera_position = nn.Parameter(
            torch.from_numpy(np.array([3.0, 6.9, +2.5],
dtype=np.float32)).to(meshes.device))

    def forward(self):
        # Render the image using the updated camera
position. Based on the new position of the
        # camera we calculate the rotation and
```

translation matrices

```
        R = look_at_rotation(self.camera_position[None,
:], device=self.device)  # (1, 3, 3)
        T = -torch.bmm(R.transpose(1, 2), self.camera_
position[None, :, None])[:, :, 0]  # (1, 3)


        image_silhouette = self.renderer_
silhouette(meshes_world=self.meshes.clone(), R=R, T=T)
        image_textured = self.renderer_textured(meshes_
world=self.meshes.clone(), R=R, T=T)


        loss_silhouette = torch.sum((image_
silhouette[..., 3] - self.image_ref_silhouette) ** 2)
        loss_texture = torch.sum((image_textured[..., :3]
- self.image_ref_textured) ** 2)


        loss = self.weight_silhouette * loss_silhouette +
self.weight_texture * loss_texture
        return loss, image_silhouette, image_textured
```

12. Next, we create an instance of the Model class and create an optimizer:

```
model = Model(meshes=cow_mesh, renderer_
silhouette=renderer_silhouette, renderer_textured =
renderer_textured,
                image_ref=image_ref, weight_silhouette=1.0,
weight_texture=0.1).to(device)

optimizer = torch.optim.Adam(model.parameters(), lr=0.05)
```

13. Finally, we run 200 optimization iterations. The rendered images are saved at each iteration:

```
for i in range(0, 200):
    if i%10 == 0:
        print('i = ', i)

    optimizer.zero_grad()
    loss, image_silhouette, image_textured = model()
    loss.backward()
    optimizer.step()
```

```
    plt.figure()
    plt.imshow(image_silhouette[..., 3].detach().
squeeze().cpu().numpy())
    plt.title("iter: %d, loss: %0.2f" % (i, loss.data))
    plt.axis("off")
    plt.savefig(os.path.join(output_dir, 'soft_
silhouette_' + str(i) + '.png'))
    plt.close()


    plt.figure()
    plt.imshow(image_textured.detach().squeeze().cpu().
numpy())
    plt.title("iter: %d, loss: %0.2f" % (i, loss.data))
    plt.axis("off")
    plt.savefig(os.path.join(output_dir, 'soft_texture_'
+ str(i) + '.png'))
    plt.close()


    R = look_at_rotation(model.camera_position[None, :],
device=model.device)
    T = -torch.bmm(R.transpose(1, 2), model.camera_
position[None, :, None])[:, :, 0]  # (1, 3)
    image = phong_renderer(meshes_world=model.meshes.
clone(), R=R, T=T)


    plt.figure()
    plt.imshow(image[..., 3].detach().squeeze().cpu().
numpy())
    plt.title("iter: %d, loss: %0.2f" % (i, loss.data))
    plt.axis("off")
    plt.savefig(os.path.join(output_dir, 'hard_
silhouette_' + str(i) + '.png'))
    plt.close()


    image = image[0, ..., :3].detach().squeeze().cpu().
numpy()
    image = img_as_ubyte(image)
```

```
    plt.figure()
    plt.imshow(image[..., :3])
    plt.title("iter: %d, loss: %0.2f" % (i, loss.data))
    plt.axis("off")
    plt.savefig(os.path.join(output_dir, 'hard_texture_'
+ str(i) + '.png'))
    plt.close()

    if loss.item() < 800:
        break
```

The observed silhouette image is shown in *Figure 4.12*:

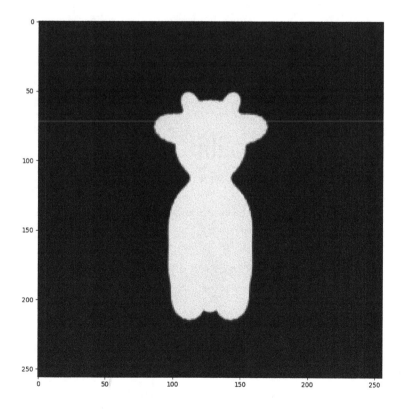

Figure 4.12: Observed silhouette image

The RGB image is shown in *Figure 4.13*:

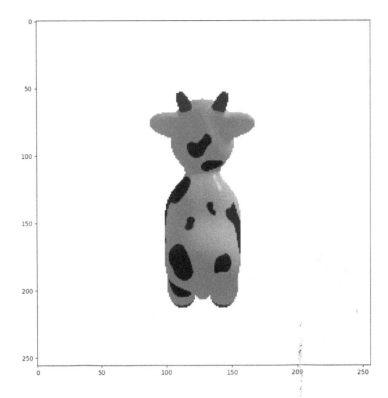

Figure 4.13: Observed RGB image

The rendered RGB images corresponding to the initial camera position and final fitted camera position are shown in *Figure 4.14* and *Figure 4.15* respectively.

iter: 0, loss: 7313.08

Figure 4.14: Image corresponding to the initial camera position

The image corresponding to the final position is as follows:

iter: 72, loss: 738.10

Figure 4.15: Image corresponding to the fitted camera position

Summary

In this chapter, we started with the question of why differentiable rendering is needed. The answers to this question lie in the fact that rendering can be considered as a mapping from 3D scenes (meshes or point clouds) to 2D images. If rendering is made differentiable, then we can optimize 3D models directly with a properly chosen cost function between the rendered images and observed images.

We then discussed an approach to make rendering differentiable, which is implemented in the PyTorch3D library. We then discussed two concrete examples of object pose estimation being formulated as an optimization problem, where the object pose is directly optimized to minimize the mean-square errors between the rendered images and observed images.

We also went through the code examples, where PyTorch3D is used to solve optimization problems. In the next chapter, we will explore more variations of differentiable rendering and where we can use it.

5

Understanding Differentiable Volumetric Rendering

In this chapter, we are going to discuss a new way of differentiable rendering. We are going to use a voxel 3D data representation, unlike the mesh 3D data representation we used in the last chapter. Voxel 3D data representation has certain advantages compared to mesh models. For example, it is more flexible and highly structured.

To understand volumetric rendering, we need to understand several important concepts, such as ray sampling, volumes, volume sampling, and ray marching. All these concepts have corresponding PyTorch3D implementations. We will discuss each of these concepts using explanations and coding exercises.

After we understand the preceding basic concepts of volumetric rendering, we can then see easily that all the operations mentioned already are already differentiable. Volumetric rendering is naturally differentiable. Thus, by then, we will be ready to use differentiable volumetric rendering for some real applications. We are going to go over a coding example of reconstructing 3D voxel models from multiple images by using differentiable volumetric rendering.

We will first understand volumetric rendering on a high level. We will then dive into the basic concepts, such as ray sampling, volumes, volume sampling, and ray marching. We will then present a coding example of reconstructing 3D object shapes from a collection of images taken from different views of the object.

In this chapter, we're going to cover the following main topics:

- A high-level description of volumetric rendering
- Understanding ray sampling
- Using volume sampling
- Understanding ray marching
- Reconstructing 3D objects and colors from multi-view images

Technical requirements

In order to run the example code snippets in this book, you need to have a computer, ideally with a GPU. However, running the code snippets with only CPUs is not impossible.

The recommended computer configuration includes the following:

- A GPU for example, the NVIDIA GTX series or RTX series with at least 8 GB of memory
- Python 3
- PyTorch library and PyTorch3D libraries

The code snippets with this chapter can be found at `https://github.com/PacktPublishing/3D-Deep-Learning-with-Python`.

Overview of volumetric rendering

Volumetric rendering is a collection of techniques used to generate a 2D view of discrete 3D data. This 3D discrete data could be a collection of images, voxel representation, or any other discrete representation of data. The main goal of volumetric rendering is to render a 2D projection of 3D data since that is what our eyes can perceive on a flat screen. This method generated such projections without any explicit conversion to a geometric representation (such as meshes). Volumetric rendering is typically used when generating surfaces is difficult or can lead to errors. It can also be used when the content (and not just the geometry and surface) of the volume is important. It is typically used for data visualization. For example, in brain scans, a visualization of the content of the interior of the brain is typically very important.

In this section, we will explore the volumetric rendering of a volume. We will get a high-level overview of volumetric rendering as shown in *Figure 5.1*:

1. First, we represent the 3D space and objects in it by using a **volume**, which is a 3D grid of regularly spaced nodes. Each node has two properties: density and color features. The density typically ranges from 0 to 1. Density can also be understood as the probability of occupancy. That is, how sure we think that the node is occupied by a certain object. In some cases, the probability can also be opacity.

2. We need to define one or multiple cameras. The rendering is the process that determines what the cameras can observe from their views.

3. To determine the RGB values at each pixel of the preceding cameras, a ray is generated from the projection center going through each image pixel of the cameras. We need to check the probability of occupancy or opacity and colors along this ray to determine RGB values for the pixel. Note there are infinitely many points on each such ray. Thus, we need to have a sampling scheme to select a certain number of points along this ray. This sampling operation is called **ray sampling**.

4. Note that we have densities and colors defined on the nodes of the volume but not on the points on the rays. Thus, we need to have a way to convert densities and colors of volumes to points on rays. This operation is called **volume sampling**.

5. Finally, from the densities and colors of the rays, we need to determine the RGB values of each pixel. In this process, we need to compute how many incident lights can arrive at each point along the ray and how many lights are reflected to the image pixel. We call this process **ray marching**.

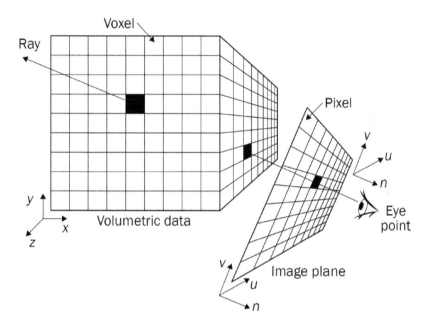

Figure 5.1: Volumetric rendering

Having understood the basic process of volumetric rendering, let us dive deeper into the first concept: ray sampling.

Understanding ray sampling

Ray sampling is the process of emitting rays from the camera that goes through the image pixels and sampling points along these rays. The ray sampling scheme depends on the use case. For example, sometimes we might want to randomly sample rays that go through some random subset of image pixels. Typically, we need to use such a sampler during training since we only need a representative sample from the full data. In such cases, we can use `MonteCarloRaysampler` in Pytorch3D. In other cases, we want to get the pixel values for each pixel on the image and maintain a spatial order. This is useful for rendering and visualization. For such use cases, PyTorch3D provides `NDCMultiNomialRaysampler`.

In the following, we will demonstrate how to use one of the PyTorch3D ray samplers, NDCGridRaysampler. This is like NDCMultiNomialRaysampler, where pixels are sampled along a grid. The codes can be found in the GitHub repository named understand_ray_sampling.py:

1. First, we need to import all the Python modules, including the definition of NDCGridRaysampler:

```
import torch
import math
import numpy as np

from pytorch3d.renderer import (
    FoVPerspectiveCameras,
    PointLights,
    look_at_view_transform,
    NDCGridRaysampler,
)
```

2. Set up the devices for use in the following steps. If we have GPUs, then we are going to use the first GPU. Otherwise, we are going to use the CPU:

```
if torch.cuda.is_available():
    device = torch.device("cuda:0")
    torch.cuda.set_device(device)
else:
    device = torch.device("cpu")
```

3. We define a batch of 10 cameras. Here, num_views is the number of views, which is 10 in this case. The elev variable denotes the elevation angle, and azim denotes the azimuth angle. The rotation, R, and translation, T, can thus be determined using the PyTorch3D look_at_view_transform function. The 10 cameras then can be defined by using rotations and translations. The 10 cameras all point at an object located at the center of the world coordinates:

```
num_views: int = 10
azimuth_range: float = 180
elev = torch.linspace(0, 0, num_views)
azim = torch.linspace(-azimuth_range, azimuth_range, num_views) + 180.0
lights = PointLights(device=device, location=[[0.0, 0.0, -3.0]])
```

```
R, T = look_at_view_transform(dist=2.7, elev=elev,
azim=azim)
cameras = FoVPerspectiveCameras(device=device, R=R, T=T)
```

4. Finally, we can define the ray sampler, which is the `raysampler` variable. We need to specify the image size of the camera. We also need to specify the minimum and maximum depths that the ray ranges from. The `n_pts_per_ray` input is the number of points along the ray:

```
image_size = 64
volume_extent_world = 3.0
raysampler = NDCGridRaysampler(
    image_width=image_size,
    image_height=image_size,
    n_pts_per_ray=50,
    min_depth=0.1,
    max_depth=volume_extent_world,
)
```

5. In the preceding step, we have already defined a ray sampler. To make the ray sampler samples rays and points for use, we need to let the ray sampler know where our cameras are and in what directions they are pointing. This can be easily achieved by passing the cameras defined in step 3 to `raysampler`. What we obtain is then a `ray_bundle` variable:

```
ray_bundle = raysampler(cameras)
```

6. The `ray_bundle` variable contains a collection of different PyTorch tensors that specify the sampled rays and points. We can print these member variables to check their shapes and verify their contents:

```
print('ray_bundle origins tensor shape = ', ray_bundle.
origins.shape)
print('ray_bundle directions shape = ', ray_bundle.
directions.shape)
print('ray_bundle lengths = ', ray_bundle.lengths.shape)
print('ray_bundle xys shape = ', ray_bundle.xys.shape)
```

7. The codes should run and print the following information:

- We can see that `ray_bundle.origins` is a tensor about the origins of the rays, and the batch size is 10. Because the image size is 64 by 64, the size of the second and third dimensions are both 64. For each origin, we need three numbers to specify its 3D location.

- `ray_bundle.directions` is a tensor about the directions of the ray. Again, the batch size is 10 and the image size is 64 by 64. These explain the size of the first three dimensions of the tensor. We need three numbers to specify a direction in 3D spaces.

- `ray_bundle.lengths` is a tensor about the depths of each point on the rays. There are 10x64x64 rays and there are 50 points on each ray.

- `ray_bundle.xys` is a tensor about the x and y locations on the image plane corresponding to each ray. There are 10x64x64 rays. We need one number to represent the x location and one number to represent the y location:

```
ray_bundle origins tensor shape =  torch.Size([10, 64,
64, 3])
ray_bundle directions shape =  torch.Size([10, 64, 64,
3])
ray_bundle lengths =  torch.Size([10, 64, 64, 50])
ray_bundle xys shape =  torch.Size([10, 64, 64, 2])
```

8. Finally, we save `ray_bundle` to a `ray_sampling.pt` file. These rays are useful for our coding exercises in the following sections:

```
torch.save({
    'ray_bundle': ray_bundle
}, 'ray_sampling.pt')
```

By now, we understand what ray samplers do. Ray samplers give us a batch of rays and discrete points on the rays. However, we still do not have densities and colors defined on these points and rays. Next, we are going to learn how to get these densities and colors from the volumes.

Using volume sampling

Volume sampling is the process of getting color and occupancy information along the points provided by the ray samples. The volume representation we are working with is discrete. Therefore, the points defined in the ray sampling step might not fall exactly on a point. The nodes of the volume grids and points on rays typically have different spatial locations. We need to use an interpolation scheme to interpolate the densities and colors at points of rays from the densities and colors at volumes. We can do that by using `VolumeSampler` implemented in PyTorch3D. The following code can be found in the GitHub repository in the `understand_volume_sampler.py` file:

1. Import the Python modules that we need:

```
import torch
from pytorch3d.structures import import Volumes
```

```
from pytorch3d.renderer.implicit.renderer import
VolumeSampler
```

2. Set up the devices:

```
if torch.cuda.is_available():
    device = torch.device("cuda:0")
    torch.cuda.set_device(device)
else:
    device = torch.device("cpu")
```

3. Load ray_bundle, which was computed in the last section:

```
checkpoint = torch.load('ray_sampling.pt')
ray_bundle = checkpoint.get('ray_bundle')
```

4. We then define a volume. The densities tensor has a shape of [10, 1, 64, 64, 50], where we have a batch of 10 volumes, and each volume is a grid of 64x64x50 nodes. Each node has one number to represent the density at the node. On the other hand, the colors tensor has a shape of [10, 3, 64, 64, 50], because each color needs three numbers to represent the RGB values:

```
batch_size = 10
densities = torch.zeros([batch_size, 1, 64, 64, 64]).
to(device)
colors = torch.zeros(batch_size, 3, 64, 64, 64).
to(device)
voxel_size = 0.1

volumes = Volumes(
    densities=densities,
    features=colors,
    voxel_size=voxel_size
)
```

5. We need to define volume_sampler based on the volumes. Here, we use bilinear interpolation for the volume sampling. The densities and colors of points on the rays can then be easily obtained by passing ray_bundle to volume_sampler:

```
volume_sampler = VolumeSampler(volumes = volumes, sample_
mode = "bilinear")
rays_densities, rays_features = volume_sampler(ray_
bundle)
```

6. We can print out the shape of the densities and colors:

```
print('rays_densities shape = ', rays_densities.shape)
print('rays_features shape = ', rays_features.shape)
```

7. The output is as follows. Note that we have a batch size of 10 cameras, which explains the size of the first dimension of the tensors. We have one ray for each image pixel and our camera image resolution is 64 by 64. The number of points on each ray is 50, which explains the size of the fourth dimension of the tensors. Each density can be represented by one number and each color needs three numbers to represent the RGB values:

```
rays_densities shape =  torch.Size([10, 64, 64, 50, 1])
rays_features shape =  torch.Size([10, 64, 64, 50, 3])
```

8. Finally, let us save the densities and colors because we need to use them in the next section:

```
torch.save({
    'rays_densities': rays_densities,
    'rays_features': rays_features
}, 'volume_sampling.pt')
```

We now have an overview of volume sampling. We know what it is and why it is useful. In the next section, we will learn about how to use these densities and colors to generate the RGB image values on the batch of cameras.

Exploring the ray marcher

Now that we have the color and density values for all the points sampled with the ray sampler, we need to figure out how to use it to finally render the pixel value on the projected image. In this section, we are going to discuss the process of converting the densities and colors on points of rays to RGB values on images. This process models the physical process of image formation.

In this section, we discuss a very simple model, where the RGB value of each image pixel is a weighted sum of the colors on the points of the corresponding ray. If we consider the densities as probabilities of occupancy or opacity, then the incident light intensity at each point of the ray is a = product of $(1-p\_i)$, where p_i are the densities. Given the probability that this point is occupied by a certain object is p_i, the expected light intensity reflected from this point is $w\_i = a \, p\_i$. We just use w_i as the weights for the weighted sum of colors. Usually, we normalize the weights by applying a softmax operation, such that the weights all sum up to one.

PyTorch3D contains multiple implementations of ray marchers. The following codes can be found in understand_ray_marcher.py in the GitHub repository:

1. In this first step, we will import all the required packages:

```
import torch
from pytorch3d.renderer.implicit.raymarching import
EmissionAbsorptionRaymarcher
```

2. Next, we load the densities and colors on rays from the last section:

```
checkpoint = torch.load('volume_sampling.pt')
rays_densities = checkpoint.get('rays_densities')
rays_features = checkpoint.get('rays_features')
```

3. We define ray_marcher and pass the densities and colors on rays to ray_marcher. This gives us image_features, which are exactly rendered RGB values:

```
ray_marcher = EmissionAbsorptionRaymarcher()
image_features = ray_marcher(rays_densities = rays_
densities, rays_features = rays_features)
```

4. We can print the image feature shape:

```
print('image_features shape = ', image_features.shape)
```

5. As we have expected, the shape is [10, 64, 64, 4], where 10 is the batch size, and 64 is the image width and height. The outputs have four channels, the first three are RGBs. The last channel is the alpha channel, which represents whether the pixel is in the foreground or the background:

```
image_features shape =  torch.Size([10, 64, 64, 4])
```

We have now gone through some of the main components of volumetric rendering. Note that the computation process from the volume densities and colors to image pixel RGB values is already differentiable. So, volumetric rendering is naturally differentiable. Given that all the variables in the preceding examples are PyTorch tensors, we can compute gradients on these variables.

In the next section, we will learn about differentiable volume rendering and see an example of using volumetric rendering for reconstructing 3D models from multi-view images.

Differentiable volumetric rendering

While standard volumetric rendering is used to render 2D projections of 3D data, differentiable volume rendering is used to do the opposite: construct 3D data from 2D images. This is how it works: we represent the shape and texture of the object as a parametric function. This function can be used to generate 2D projections. But, given 2D projections (this is typically multiple views of the 3D scene), we can optimize the parameters of these implicit shape and texture functions so that its projections are the multi-view 2D images. This optimization is possible since the rendering process is completely differentiable, and the implicit functions used are also differentiable.

Reconstructing 3D models from multi-view images

In this section, we are going to show an example of using differentiable volumetric rendering for reconstructing 3D models from multi-view images. Reconstructing 3D models is a frequently sought problem. Usually, the direct ways of measuring the 3D world are difficult and costly, for example, LiDAR and Radar are typically expensive. On the other hand, 2D cameras have much lower costs, which makes reconstructing the 3D world from 2D images incredibly attractive. Of course, to reconstruct the 3D world, we need multiple images from multiple views.

The following `volume_renderer.py` code can be found in the GitHub repository and it is modified from a tutorial of PyTorch3D. We will use this coding example to show how the real-world application of volumetric rendering can be:

1. First, we need to import all the Python modules:

    ```
    import os
    import sys
    import time
    import json
    import glob
    import torch
    import math
    import matplotlib.pyplot as plt
    import numpy as np
    from PIL import Image

    from pytorch3d.structures import Volumes
    from pytorch3d.renderer import (
        FoVPerspectiveCameras,
        VolumeRenderer,
        NDCGridRaysampler,
    ```

```
            EmissionAbsorptionRaymarcher
    )
    from pytorch3d.transforms import so3_exp_map

    from plot_image_grid import image_grid
    from generate_cow_renders import generate_cow_renders
```

2. Next, we need to set up the device:

```
    if torch.cuda.is_available():
        device = torch.device("cuda:0")
        torch.cuda.set_device(device)
    else:
        device = torch.device("cpu")
```

3. Using the provided function from the PyTorch3D tutorial, we generate 40 cameras, images, and silhouette images with different angles. We will consider these images as the given ground-truth images, and we will fit a 3D volumetric model to these observed ground-truth images:

```
    target_cameras, target_images, target_silhouettes =
    generate_cow_renders(num_views=40)
```

4. Next, we define a ray sampler. As we have discussed in the previous sections, the ray sampler is for sample rays, and points per rays for us:

```
    render_size = 128
    volume_extent_world = 3.0

    raysampler = NDCGridRaysampler(
        image_width=render_size,
        image_height=render_size,
        n_pts_per_ray=150,
        min_depth=0.1,
        max_depth=volume_extent_world,
    )
```

5. Next, we create the ray marcher as before. Note, this time, we define a variable renderer of the `VolumeRenderer` type. `VolumeRenderer` is just a nice interface, where ray samplers and ray marchers do all the heavy-lifting work under the hood:

```
raymarcher = EmissionAbsorptionRaymarcher()
renderer = VolumeRenderer(
    raysampler=raysampler, raymarcher=raymarcher,
)
```

6. Next, we define a `VolumeModel` class. This class is just for encapsulating a volume so that the gradients can be computed in the forward function and the volume densities and colors can be updated by the optimizer:

```
class VolumeModel(torch.nn.Module):
    def __init__(self, renderer, volume_size=[64] * 3,
voxel_size=0.1):
        super().__init__()
        self.log_densities = torch.nn.Parameter(-4.0 *
torch.ones(1, *volume_size))
        self.log_colors = torch.nn.Parameter(torch.
zeros(3, *volume_size))
        self._voxel_size = voxel_size
        self._renderer = renderer

    def forward(self, cameras):
        batch_size = cameras.R.shape[0]

        densities = torch.sigmoid(self.log_densities)
        colors = torch.sigmoid(self.log_colors)

        volumes = Volumes(
            densities=densities[None].expand(
                batch_size, *self.log_densities.shape),
            features=colors[None].expand(
                batch_size, *self.log_colors.shape),
            voxel_size=self._voxel_size,
        )
        return self._renderer(cameras=cameras,
volumes=volumes)[0]
```

7. Define a Huber loss function. The Huber loss function is a robust loss function to prevent a small number of outliers from dragging the optimization away from the true optimal solutions. Minimizing this loss function will move x closer to y:

```
def huber(x, y, scaling=0.1):
    diff_sq = (x - y) ** 2
    loss = ((1 + diff_sq / (scaling ** 2)).clamp(1e-4).
sqrt() - 1) * float(scaling)
    return loss
```

8. Move everything to the right device:

```
target_cameras = target_cameras.to(device)
target_images = target_images.to(device)
target_silhouettes = target_silhouettes.to(device)
```

9. Define an instance of VolumeModel:

```
volume_size = 128
volume_model = VolumeModel(
    renderer,
    volume_size=[volume_size] * 3,
    voxel_size=volume_extent_world / volume_size,
).to(device)
```

10. Now let's set up the optimizer. The learning rate, lr, is set to 0.1. We use an Adam optimizer, and the number of optimization iterations will be 300:

```
lr = 0.1
optimizer = torch.optim.Adam(volume_model.parameters(),
lr=lr)
batch_size = 10
n_iter = 300
```

11. Next, we have the main optimization loop. The densities and colors of the volume are rendered, and the resulting colors and silhouettes are compared with the observed multi-view images. The Huber loss between the rendered images and observed ground-truth images is minimized:

```
for iteration in range(n_iter):

    if iteration == round(n_iter * 0.75):
        print('Decreasing LR 10-fold ...')
```

```
        optimizer = torch.optim.Adam(
            volume_model.parameters(), lr=lr * 0.1
        )

    optimizer.zero_grad()
    batch_idx = torch.randperm(len(target_cameras))
[:batch_size]

    # Sample the minibatch of cameras.
    batch_cameras = FoVPerspectiveCameras(
        R=target_cameras.R[batch_idx],
        T=target_cameras.T[batch_idx],
        znear=target_cameras.znear[batch_idx],
        zfar=target_cameras.zfar[batch_idx],
        aspect_ratio=target_cameras.aspect_ratio[batch_
idx],
        fov=target_cameras.fov[batch_idx],
        device=device,
    )

    rendered_images, rendered_silhouettes = volume_model(
        batch_cameras
    ).split([3, 1], dim=-1)

    sil_err = huber(
        rendered_silhouettes[..., 0], target_
silhouettes[batch_idx],
    ).abs().mean()

    color_err = huber(
        rendered_images, target_images[batch_idx],
    ).abs().mean()

    loss = color_err + sil_err
    loss.backward()
    optimizer.step()
```

12. After the optimization is finished, we take the final resulting volumetric model and render images from new angles:

```
with torch.no_grad():
  rotating_volume_frames = ge erate_rotating_
volume(volume_model, n_frames=7 * 4)

image_grid(rotating_volume_frames.clamp(0., 1. .cpu().
numpy(), rows=4, cols=7, rgb=True, fill=True)
plt.savefig('rotating_volume.png')
plt.show()
```

13. Finally, the rendered new images are shown in Figure 5.2:

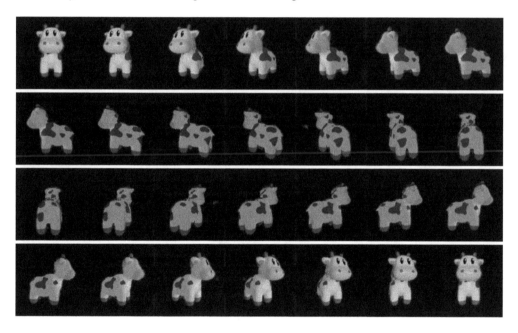

Figure 5.2: Rendered images from the fitted 3D model

By now, we have an overview of some of the main concepts in differentiable volumetric rendering. We have also learned a concrete example of using differentiable volumetric rendering for reconstructing 3D models from multiview images. You should be able to master the skills already and be able to use the technique for your own problems.

Summary

In this chapter, we started with a high-level description of differentiable volumetric rendering. We then dived deep into several important concepts of differentiable volumetric rendering, including ray sampling, volume sampling, and the ray marcher, but only by explanations and coding examples. We walked through a coding example of using differentiable volumetric rendering for reconstructing 3D models from multi-view images.

Using volumes for 3D deep learning has become an interesting direction in recent years. As many innovative ideas come out following this direction, many breakthroughs are emerging. One of the breakthroughs, called **Neural Radiance Fields** (**NeRF**), will be the topic of our next chapter.

6

Exploring Neural Radiance Fields (NeRF)

In the previous chapter, you learned about Differentiable Volume Rendering where you reconstructed the 3D volume from several multi-view images. With this technique, you modeled a volume consisting of N x N x N voxels. The space requirement for storing this volume scale would therefore be $O(N^3)$. This is undesirable, especially if we want to transmit this information over the network. Other methods can overcome such large disk space requirements, but they are prone to smoothing geometry and texture. Therefore, we cannot use them to model very complex or textured scenes reliably.

In this chapter, we are going to discuss a breakthrough new approach to representing 3D scenes, called **Neural Radiance Fields** (**NeRF**). This is one of the first techniques to model a 3D scene that requires less constant disk space and at the same time, captures the fine geometry and texture of complex scenes.

In this chapter, you will learn about the following topics:

- Understanding NeRF

- Training a NeRF model

- Understanding the NeRF model architecture

- Understanding volume rendering with radiance fields

Technical requirements

In order to run the example code snippets in this book, you need to have a computer, ideally with a GPU with about 8 GB of GPU memory. Running code snippets only using CPUs is not impossible but will be extremely slow. The recommended computer configuration is as follows:

- A GPU device – for example, Nvidia GTX series or RTX series with at least 8 GB of memory

- Python 3.7+

- The PyTorch and PyTorch3D libraries

The code snippets for this chapter can be found at `https://github.com/PacktPublishing/3D-Deep-Learning-with-Python`.

Understanding NeRF

View synthesis is a long-standing problem in 3D computer vision. The challenge is to synthesize new views of a 3D scene using a small number of available 2D snapshots of the scene. It is particularly challenging because the view of a complex scene can depend on a lot of factors such as object artifacts, light sources, reflections, opacity, object surface texture, and occlusions. Any good representation should capture this information either implicitly or explicitly. Additionally, many objects have complex structures that are not completely visible from a certain viewpoint. The challenge is to construct complete information about the world given incomplete and noisy information.

As the name suggests, NeRF uses neural networks to model the world. As we will learn later in the chapter, NeRF uses neural networks in a very unconventional manner. It was a concept first developed by a team of researchers from UC Berkeley, Google Research, and UC San Diego. Because of their unconventional use of neural networks and the quality of the learned models, it has spawned multiple new inventions in the fields of view synthesis, depth sensing, and 3D reconstruction. It is therefore a very useful concept to understand as you navigate through the rest of this chapter and book.

In this section, first, we will explore the meaning of radiance fields and how we can use a neural network to represent these radiance fields.

What is a radiance field?

Before we get to NeRF, let us understand what radiance fields are first. You see an object when the light from that object is processed by your body's sensory system. The light from the object can either be generated by the object itself or reflected off it.

Radiance is the standard metric for measuring the amount of light that passes through or is emitted from an area inside a particular solid angle. For our purposes, we can treat the radiance to be the intensity of a point in space when viewed in a particular direction. When capturing this information in RGB, the radiance will have three components corresponding to the colors Red, Green, and Blue. The radiance of a point in space can depend on many factors, including the following:

- Light sources illuminating that point
- The existence of a surface (or volume density) that can reflect light at that point
- The texture properties of the surface

The following figure depicts the radiance value at a certain point in the 3D scene when viewed at a certain angle. The radiance field is just a collection of these radiance values at all points and viewing angles in the 3D scene:

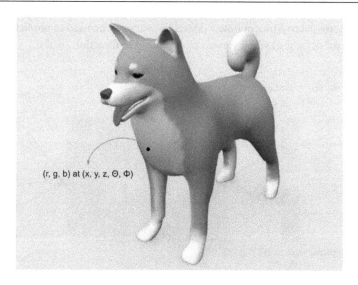

Figure 6.1: The radiance (r, g, b) at a point (x, y, z) when viewed with certain viewing angles (θ, Ø)

If we know the radiance of all the points in a scene in all directions, we have all the visual information we need about the scene. This field of radiance values constitutes a radiance field. We can store the radiance field information as a volume in a 3D voxel grid data structure. We saw this in the previous chapter when discussing volume rendering.

Representing radiance fields with neural networks

In this section, we will explore a new way of using neural networks. In typical computer vision tasks, we use neural networks to map an input in the pixel space to an output. In the case of a discriminative model, the output is a class label. In the case of a generative model, the output is also in the pixel space. A NeRF model is neither of these.

NeRF uses a neural network to represent a volumetric scene function. This neural network takes a 5-dimensional input. These are the three spatial locations (x, y, z) and two viewing angles (θ, Ø). Its output is the volume density σ at (x, y, z) and the emitted color (r, g, b) of the point (x, y, z) when viewed from the viewing angle (θ, Ø). The emitted color is a proxy used to estimate the radiance at that point. In practice, instead of directly using (θ, Ø) to represent the viewing angle, NeRF uses the unit direction vector d in the 3D Cartesian coordinate system. These are equivalent representations of the viewing angle.

The model therefore maps any point in the 3D scene and a viewing angle to the volume density and radiance at that point. You can then use this model to synthesize views by querying the 5D coordinates along camera rays and using the volume rendering technique you learned about in the previous chapter to project the output colors and volume densities into an image.

With the following figure, let us find out how a neural network can be used to predict the density and radiance at a certain point (x, y, z) when viewed along a certain direction (θ, Ø):

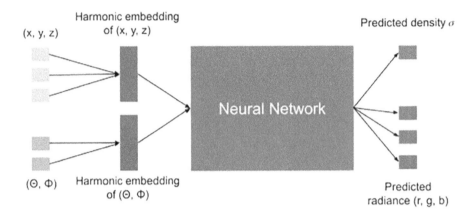

Figure 6.2: The inputs (x, y, z, θ, and Ø) are used to create separate harmonic embeddings
for the spatial location and viewing angle first, forming the input to a neural network,
and this neural network outputs the predicted density and radiance

Note that this is a fully connected network – typically, this is referred to as a **Multi-Layer Perceptron** (**MLP**). More importantly, this is not a convolutional neural network. We refer to this model as the NeRF model. A single NeRF model is optimized on a set of images from a single scene. Therefore, each model only knows the scene on which it is optimized. This is not the standard way to use a neural network, where we typically need the model to generalize unseen images. In the case of NeRF, we need the network to generalize unseen viewpoints well.

Now that you know what a NeRF is, let us look at how to use it to render new views from it.

Training a NeRF model

In this section, we are going to train a simple NeRF model on images generated from the synthetic cow model. We are only going to instantiate the NeRF model without worrying about how it is implemented. The implementation details are covered in the next section. A single neural network (NeRF model) is trained to represent a single 3D scene. The following codes can be found in `train_nerf.py`, which can be found in this chapter's GitHub repository. It is modified from a PyTorch3D tutorial. Let us go through the code to train a NeRF model on the synthetic cow scene:

1. First, let us import the standard modules:

    ```
    import torch
    import matplotlib.pyplot as plt
    ```

2. Next, let us import the functions and classes used for rendering. These are `pytorch3d` data structures:

```
from pytorch3d.renderer import (
FoVPerspectiveCameras,
NDCMultinomialRaysampler,
MonteCarloRaysampler,
EmissionAbsorptionRaymarcher,
ImplicitRenderer,
)
from utils.helper_functions import (generate_rotating_
nerf,
huber,
sample_images_at_mc_locs)
from nerf_model import NeuralRadianceField
```

3. Next, we need to set up the device:

```
if torch.cuda.is_available():
    device = torch.device("cuda:0")
    torch.cuda.set_device(device)
else:
    device = torch.device("cpu")
```

4. Next, let us import the utility functions that will let us generate synthetic training data and visualize images:

```
from utils.plot_image_grid import image_grid
from utils.generate_cow_renders import generate_cow_
renders
```

5. We can now use these utility functions to generate camera angles, images, and silhouettes of the synthetic cow from multiple different angles. This will print the number of generated images, silhouettes, and camera angles:

```
target_cameras, target_images, target_silhouettes =
generate_cow_renders(num_views=40, azimuth_range=180)
print(f'Generated {len(target_images)} images/
silhouettes/cameras.')
```

6. As we have done in the previous chapter, let us define a ray sampler. We will use `MonteCarloRaysampler`. This generates rays from a random subset of pixels from the image plane. We need a random sampler here since we want to use a mini-batch gradient descent algorithm to optimize the model. This is a standard neural network optimization technique. Sampling rays systematically can result in optimization bias during each optimization step. This can lead to a worse model and increase the model training time. The ray sampler samples points uniformly along the ray:

```
render_size = target_images.shape[1] * 2
volume_extent_world = 3.0
raysampler_mc = MonteCarloRaysampler(
    min_x = -1.0,
    max_x = 1.0,
    min_y = -1.0,
    max_y = 1.0,
    n_rays_per_image=750,
    n_pts_per_ray=128,
    min_depth=0.1,
    max_depth=volume_extent_world,
)
```

7. Next, we will define the ray marcher. This uses the volume densities and colors of points sampled along the ray and renders the pixel value for that ray. For the ray marcher, we use `EmissionAbsorptionRaymarcher`. This implements the classical Emission-Absorption ray marching algorithm:

```
raymarcher = EmissionAbsorptionRaymarcher()
```

8. We will now instantiate `ImplicitRenderer`. This composes the ray sampler and the ray marcher into a single data structure:

```
renderer_mc = ImplicitRenderer(raysampler=raysampler_mc,
raymarcher=raymarcher)
```

9. Let us look at the Huber loss function. This is defined in `utils.helper_functions.huber`. It is a robust alternative to the mean squared error function and is less sensitive to outliers:

```
def huber(x, y, scaling=0.1):
    diff_sq = (x - y) ** 2
    loss = ((1 + diff_sq / (scaling**2)).clamp(1e-4).
sqrt() - 1) * float(scaling)
    return loss
```

10. We will now look at a helper function defined in utils.helper_functions.sample_ images_at_mc_loss that is used to extract ground truth pixel values from target images. MonteCarloRaysampler samples rays passing through some x and y locations on the image. These are in **Normalized Device Coordinates (NDCs)**. However, we need to sample from the image pixel coordinates. For this, we use the torch.nn.functional.grid_sample function. This uses interpolation techniques in the background to provide us with accurate pixel values. This is better than just mapping NDC coordinates to pixel coordinates and then sampling the one pixel that corresponds to an NDC coordinate value. In the NDC coordinate system, x and y both have a range of [-1, 1]. For example, (x, y) = (-1, -1) corresponds to the top left corner of the image:

```
def sample_images_at_mc_locs(target_images, sampled_rays_
xy):
    ba = target_images.shape[0]
    dim = target_images.shape[-1]
    spatial_size = sampled_rays_xy.shape[1:-1]
    images_sampled = torch.nn.functional.grid_sample(
        target_images.permute(0, 3, 1, 2),
        -sampled_rays_xy.view(ba, -1, 1, 2),  # note the
sign inversion
        align_corners=True
    )
    return images_sampled.permute(0, 2, 3, 1).view(
        ba, *spatial_size, dim
    )
```

11. While training the model, it is always useful to visualize the model output. Among many other uses, this will help us course-correct if we see that the model outputs are not changing over time. So far, we have used MonteCarloRaysampler, which is very useful while training the model, but this will not be useful when we want to render full images since it randomly samples rays. To view the full image, we need to systematically sample rays corresponding to all the pixels in the output frame. To achieve this, we are going to use NDCMultinomialRaysampler:

```
render_size = target_images.shape[1] * 2
volume_extent_world = 3.0
raysampler_grid = NDCMultinomialRaysampler(
    image_height=render_size,
    image_width=render_size,
    n_pts_per_ray=128,
    min_depth=0.1,
```

```
      max_depth=volume_extent_world,
)
```

12. We will now instantiate the implicit renderer:

```
renderer_grid = ImplicitRenderer(
    raysampler=raysampler_grid, raymarcher=raymarcher,
)
```

13. In order to visualize the intermediate training results, let us define a helper function that takes the model and camera parameters as its input and compares it with the target image and its corresponding silhouette. If the rendered image is very large, it might not be possible to fit all the rays into the GPU memory at once. Therefore, we need to break them down into batches and run several forward passes on the model to get the output. We need to merge the output of the rendering into one coherent image. In order to keep it simple, we will just import the function here, but the full code is provided in the book's GitHub repository:

```
from utils.helper_function import show_full_render
```

14. We will now instantiate the NeRF model. To keep it simple, we are not presenting the model's class definition here. You can find that in the chapter's GitHub repository. Because the model structure is so important, we are going to discuss it in detail in a separate section:

```
from nerf_model import NeuralRadianceField
neural_radiance_field = NeuralRadianceField()
```

15. Let us now prepare to train the model. In order to reproduce the training, we should set the random seed used in torch to a fixed value. We then need to send all the variables to the device used for processing. Since this is a resource-intensive computational problem, we should ideally run it on a GPU-enabled machine. Running this on a CPU is extremely time-consuming and not recommended:

```
torch.manual_seed(1)

renderer_grid = renderer_grid.to(device)
renderer_mc = renderer_mc.to(device)
target_cameras = target_cameras.to(device)
target_images = target_images.to(device)
target_silhouettes = target_silhouettes.to(device)
neural_radiance_field = neural_radiance_field.to(device)
```

16. We will now define the hyperparameters used to train the model. `lr` represents the learning rate, `n_iter` represents the number of training iterations (or steps), and `batch_size` represents the number of random cameras used in a mini-batch. The batch size here is chosen according to the GPU memory you have. If you find that you are running out of GPU memory, choose a smaller batch size value:

```
lr = 1e-3
optimizer = torch.optim.Adam(neural_radiance_field.
parameters(), lr=lr)
batch_size = 6
n_iter = 3000
```

17. We are now ready to train our model. During each iteration, we should sample a mini-batch of cameras randomly:

```
loss_history_color, loss_history_sil = [], []
for iteration in range(n_iter):
    if iteration == round(n_iter * 0.75):
        print('Decreasing LR 10-fold ...')
        optimizer = torch.optim.Adam(
            neural_radiance_field.parameters(), lr=lr *
0.1
        )
    optimizer.zero_grad()
    batch_idx = torch.randperm(len(target_cameras))
[:batch_size]
    batch_cameras = FoVPerspectiveCameras(
        R = target_cameras.R[batch_idx],
        T = target_cameras.T[batch_idx],
        znear = target_cameras.znear[batch_idx],
        zfar = target_cameras.zfar[batch_idx],
        aspect_ratio = target_cameras.aspect_ratio[batch_
idx],
        fov = target_cameras.fov[batch_idx],
        device = device,
    )
```

18. During each iteration, first, we need to obtain the rendered pixel values and rendered silhouettes at the randomly sampled cameras using the NeRF model. These are predicted values. This is the forward propagation step. We want to compare these predictions to the ground truth to find out the training loss. Our loss is a mixture of two loss functions: A, a Huber loss on the predicted silhouette and the ground truth silhouette, and B, a Huber loss on the predicted color and the ground truth color. Once we obtain the loss value, we can backpropagate through the NeRF model and step through the optimizer:

```
rendered_images_silhouettes, sampled_rays = renderer_
mc(
    cameras=batch_cameras,
    volumetric_function=neural_radiance_field
)
rendered_images, rendered_silhouettes = (
    rendered_images_silhouettes.split([3, 1], dim=-1)
)

silhouettes_at_rays = sample_images_at_mc_locs(
    target_silhouettes[batch_idx, ..., None],
    sampled_rays.xys
)
sil_err = huber(
    rendered_silhouettes,
    silhouettes_at_rays,
).abs().mean()
colors_at_rays = sample_images_at_mc_locs(
    target_images[batch_idx],
    sampled_rays.xys
)
color_err = huber(
    rendered_images,
    colors_at_rays,
).abs().mean()
```

```
    loss = color_err + sil_err
    loss_history_color.append(float(color_err))
    loss_history_sil.append(float(sil_err))

    loss.backward()
    optimizer.step()
```

19. Let us visualize model performance after every 100 iterations. This will help us track model progress and terminate it if something unexpected is happening. This creates images in the same folder where you run the code:

```
    if iteration % 100 == 0:
        show_idx = torch.randperm(len(target_cameras))
[:1]
        fig = show_full_render(
        neural_radiance_field,
        FoVPerspectiveCameras(
            R = target_cameras.R[show_idx],
            T = target_cameras.T[show_idx],
            znear = target_cameras.znear[show_idx],
            zfar = target_cameras.zfar[show_idx],
            aspect_ratio = target_cameras.aspect_
ratio[show_idx],
            fov = target_cameras.fov[show_idx],
            device = device),
        target_images[show_idx][0],
        target_silhouettes[show_idx][0],
        renderer_grid,
        loss_history_color,
        loss_history_sil)
    fig.savefig(f'intermediate_{iteration}')
```

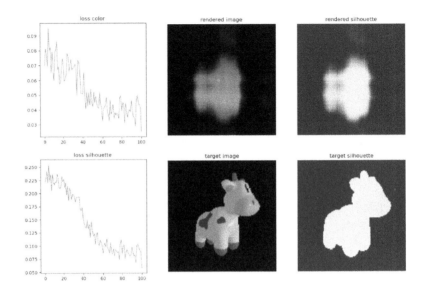

Figure 6.3: An intermediate visualization to keep track of model training

20. After the optimization is finished, we take the final resulting volumetric model and render images from new angles:

```
from utils import generate_rotating_nerf
with torch.no_grad():
    rotating_nerf_frames = generate_rotating_nerf(neural_
radiance_field, n_frames=3*5)

image_grid(rotating_nerf_frames.clamp(0., 1.).cpu().
numpy(), rows=3, cols=5, rgb=True, fill=True)
plt.show()
```

Finally, the new rendered images are shown in the figure here:

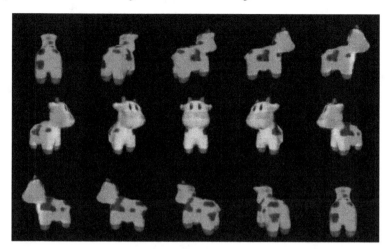

Figure 6.4: Rendered images of the synthetic cow scene that our NeRF model learned

We trained a NeRF model on a synthetic cow scene in this section. In the next section, we will learn more about how the NeRF model is implemented by going through the code in more detail.

Understanding the NeRF model architecture

So far, we have used the NeRF model class without fully knowing what it looks like. In this section, we will first visualize what the neural network looks like and then go through the code in detail and understand how it is implemented.

The neural network takes the harmonic embedding of the spatial location (x, y, z) and the harmonic embedding of $(\theta, \emptyset)$ as its input and outputs the predicted density σ and the predicted color (r, g, b). The following figure illustrates the network architecture that we are going to implement in this section:

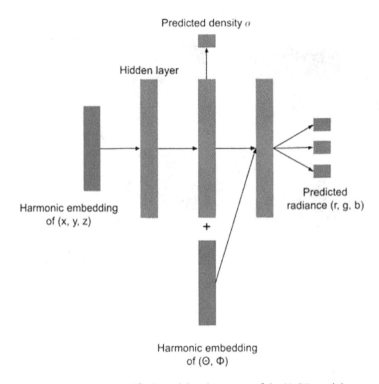

Predicted density o

Hidden layer

Harmonic embedding
of (x, y, z)

Predicted
radiance (r, g, b)

+

Harmonic embedding
of (Θ, Φ)

Figure 6.5: The simplified model architecture of the NeRF model

> **Note**
>
> The model architecture that we are going to implement is different from the original NeRF model architecture. In this implementation, we are implementing a simplified version of it. This simplified architecture makes it faster and easier to train.

Let us start defining the `NeuralRadianceField` class. We will now go through different parts of this class definition. For the full definition of the class, please refer to the code in the GitHub repository:

1. Each input point is a 5-dimensional vector. It was found that training the model directly on this input performs poorly when representing high-frequency variation in color and geometry. This is because neural networks are known to be biased toward learning low-frequency functions. A good solution to this problem is to map the input space to a higher dimensional space and use that for training. This mapping function is a set of sinusoidal functions with fixed but unique frequencies:

$$\gamma(p) = \left(\sin\left(2^0 \pi p\right), \cos\left(2^0 \pi p\right), \cdots, \sin\left(2^{L-1} \pi p\right), \cos\left(2^{L-1} \pi p\right) \right).$$

2. This function is applied to each of the components of the input vector:

```
class NeuralRadianceField(torch.nn.Module):
    def __init__(self, n_harmonic_functions=60, n_hidden_
neurons=256):
        super().__init__()
        self.harmonic_embedding = HarmonicEmbedding(n_
harmonic_functions)
```

3. The neural network consists of an MLP backbone. It takes the embeddings of location (x, y, z) as its input. This is a fully connected network and the activation function used is `softplus`. The `softplus` function is a smoother version of the ReLU activation function. The output of the backbone is a vector with a size of n_hidden_neurons:

```
        embedding_dim = n_harmonic_functions * 2 * 3
        self.mlp = torch.nn.Sequential(
            torch.nn.Linear(embedding_dim, n_hidden_
neurons),
            torch.nn.Softplus(beta=10.0),
            torch.nn.Linear(n_hidden_neurons, n_hidden_
neurons),
            torch.nn.Softplus(beta=10.0),
        )
```

4. We define a color layer that takes the output embeddings of the MLP backbone along with the ray direction input embeddings and outputs the RGB color of the input. We combine these inputs because the color output depends strongly on both the location of the point and the direction of viewing and therefore, it is important to provide shorter paths to make use of this neural network:

```
        self.color_layer = torch.nn.Sequential(
            torch.nn.Linear(n_hidden_neurons + embedding_
dim, n_hidden_neurons),
            torch.nn.Softplus(beta=10.0),
            torch.nn.Linear(n_hidden_neurons, 3),
            torch.nn.Sigmoid(),
        )
```

5. Next, we define the density layer. The density of a point is just a function of its location:

```
        self.density_layer = torch.nn.Sequential(
            torch.nn.Linear(n_hidden_neurons, 1),
```

```
            torch.nn.Softplus(beta=10.0),
        self.density_layer[0].bias.data[0] = -1.5
```

6. Now, we need some function to take the output of `density_layer` and predict the raw density:

```
def _get_densities(self, features):
    raw_densities = self.density_layer(features)
    return 1 - (-raw_densities).exp()
```

7. We do the same for obtaining colors at a certain point given the ray direction. We need to apply the positional encoding function to the ray direction input first. We should then concatenate it with the output of the MLP backbone:

```
def _get_colors(self, features, rays_directions):
    spatial_size = features.shape[:-1]
    rays_directions_normed = torch.nn.functional.
normalize(
        rays_directions, dim=-1
    )
    rays_embedding = self.harmonic_embedding(
        rays_directions_normed
    )
    rays_embedding_expand = rays_embedding[..., None,
:].expand(
        *spatial_size, rays_embedding.shape[-1]
    )
    color_layer_input = torch.cat(
        (features, rays_embedding_expand),
        dim=-1
    )
    return self.color_layer(color_layer_input)
```

8. We define the function for forward propagation. First, we obtain embeddings. Then, we pass them through the MLP backbone to obtain a set of features. We then use that to obtain the densities. We use the features and the ray directions to obtain the color. We return the densities and colors:

```
def forward(
    self,
```

```
        ray_bundle: RayBundle,
        **kwargs,
    ):
        rays_points_world = ray_bundle_to_ray_points(ray_
bundle)
        embeds = self.harmonic_embedding(
            rays_points_world
        )
        features = self.mlp(embeds)
        rays_densities = self._get_densities(features)
        # rays_densities.shape = [minibatch x ... x 1]

        rays_colors = self._get_colors(features, ray_
bundle.directions)
        return rays_densities, rays_colors
```

9. This function is used to allow for memory-efficient processing of input rays. First, the input rays are split into n_batches chunks and passed through the self.forward function one at a time in a for loop. Combined with disabling PyTorch gradient caching (torch.no_grad()), this allows us to render large batches of rays that do not all fit into GPU memory in a single forward pass. In our case, batched_forward is used to export a fully sized render of the radiance field for visualization purposes:

```
    def batched_forward(
        self,
        ray_bundle: RayBundle,
        n_batches: int = 16,
        **kwargs,
    ):
        n_pts_per_ray = ray_bundle.lengths.shape[-1]
        spatial_size = [*ray_bundle.origins.shape[:-1],
n_pts_per_ray]
        # Split the rays to `n_batches` batches.
        tot_samples = ray_bundle.origins.shape[:-1].
numel()
        batches = torch.chunk(torch.arange(tot_samples),
n_batches)
```

10. For each batch, we need to run a forward pass first and then extract the `ray_densities` and `ray_colors` separately to be returned as the outputs:

```
batch_outputs = [
    self.forward(
        RayBundle(
            origins=ray_bundle.origins.view(-1,
3)[batch_idx],
            directions=ray_bundle.directions.view(-
1, 3)[batch_idx],
            lengths=ray_bundle.lengths.view(-1,
n_pts_per_ray)[batch_idx],
            xys=None,
        )
    ) for batch_idx in batches
]
rays_densities, rays_colors = [
    torch.cat(
        [batch_output[output_i] for batch_output
in batch_outputs], dim=0
    ).view(*spatial_size, -1) for output_i in (0,
1)]
return rays_densities, rays_colors
```

In this section, we went through the implementation of the NeRF model. To get a complete understanding of NeRF, we also need to explore the theoretical concepts underlying its use in rendering volumes. In the next section, we will explore this in more detail.

Understanding volume rendering with radiance fields

Volume rendering allows you to create a 2D projection of a 3D image or scene. In this section, we will learn about rendering a 3D scene from different viewpoints. For the purposes of this section, assume that the NeRF model is fully trained and that it accurately maps the input coordinates (x, y, z, d_x, d_y, d_z) to an output (r, g, b, σ). Here are the definitions of these input and output coordinates:

- **(x, y, z)**: A point in the 3D scene in the World Coordinates

- **(dx, dy, dz)**: This is a unit vector that represents the direction along which we are viewing the point (x, y, z)

- **(r, g, b)**: This is the radiance value (or the emitted color) of the point (x, y, z)

- σ: The volume density at the point (x, y, z)

In the previous chapter, you came to understand the concepts underlying volumetric rendering. You used the technique of ray sampling to get volume densities and colors from the volume. We called this volume sampling. In this chapter, we are going to use ray sampling on the radiance field to get the volume densities and colors. We can then perform ray marching to obtain the color intensities of that point. The ray marching technique used in the previous chapter and what is used in this chapter are conceptually similar. The difference is that 3D voxels are discrete representations of 3D space whereas radiance fields are a continuous representation of it (because we use a neural network to encode this representation). This slightly changes the way we accumulate color intensities along a ray.

Projecting rays into the scene

Imagine placing a camera at a viewpoint and pointing it towards the 3D scene of interest. This is the scene on which the NeRF model is trained. To synthesize a 2D projection of the scene, we first send out of ray into the 3D scene originating from the viewpoint.

The ray can be parameterized as follows:

$$r(t) = o + td$$

Here, r is the ray starting from the origin o and traveling along the direction d. It is parametrized by t, which can be varied in order to move to different points on the ray. Note that r is a 3D vector representing a point in space.

Accumulating the color of a ray

We can use some well-known classical color rendering techniques to render the color of the ray. Before we do that, let us get a feeling for some standard definitions:

- Let us assume that we want to accumulate the color of the ray between tn (the near bound) and tf (the far bound). We do not care about the ray outside of these bounds.

- We can think of volume density $\sigma(r(t))$ as the probability that the ray terminates at an infinitesimal point around r(t).

- We can think of $c(r(t), d)$ as the color at the point r(t) on the ray when viewed in along direction d.

- $\int_{tn}^{t} \sigma(r(s))ds$ will measure the accumulated volume density between tn and some point t.

- $T(t) = \exp(-\int_{tn}^{t} \sigma(r(s))ds)$ will provide us with a notion of accumulated transmittance along the ray from tn to some point t. The higher the accumulated volume density, the lower the accumulated transmittance to the point t.

- The expected color of the ray can now be defined as follows:

$$C(\boldsymbol{r}) = \int_{tn}^{tf} T(t) * \sigma(\mathbf{r}(s)) * c(\boldsymbol{r}(t), d) * dt$$

> **Important note**
>
> The volume density $\sigma(r(t))$ is a function of the point r(t). Most notably, this does not depend on the direction vector d. This is because volume density is a function of the physical location at which the point is located. The color $c(\boldsymbol{r}(t), d)$ is a function of both the point r(t) and the ray direction d. This is because the same point in space can have different colors when viewed from different directions.

Our NeRF model is a continuous function representing the radiance field of the scene. We can use it to obtain c(r(t), d) and $\sigma(r(t))$ at various points along the ray. There are many techniques for numerically estimating the integral C(r). While training and visualizing the outputs of the NeRF model, we used the standard `EmissionAbsorptionRaymarcher` method to accumulate the radiance along a ray.

Summary

In this chapter, we came to understand how a neural network can be used to model and represent a 3D scene. This neural network is called the NeRF model. We then trained a simple NeRF model on a synthetic 3D scene. We then dug deeper into the NeRF model architecture and its implementation in code. We also understood the main components of the model. We then understood the principles behind rendering volumes with the NeRF model. The NeRF model is used to capture a single scene. Once we build this model, we can use it to render that 3D scene from different angles. It is logical to wonder whether there is a way to capture multiple scenes with a single model and whether we can predictably manipulate certain objects and attributes in the scene. This is our topic of exploration in the next chapter where we will explore the GIRAFFE model.

PART 3: State-of-the-art 3D Deep Learning Using PyTorch3D

This part of the book will be all about using PyTorch3D to implement state-of-the-art 3D deep learning models and algorithms. 3D computer vision technologies are making rapid progress in recent times and we will learn how to implement and use these state-of-the-art 3D deep learning models in the best way possible.

This part includes the following chapter:

- *Chapter 7, Exploring Controllable Neural Feature Fields*
- *Chapter 8, Modeling the Human Body in 3D*
- *Chapter 9, Performing End-to-End View Synthesis with SynSin*
- *Chapter 10, Mesh R-CNN*

7
Exploring Controllable Neural Feature Fields

In the previous chapter, you learned how to represent a 3D scene using **Neural Radiance Fields** (**NeRF**). We trained a single neural network on posed multi-view images of a 3D scene to learn an implicit representation of it. Then, we used the NeRF model to render the 3D scene from various other viewpoints and viewing angles. With this model, we assumed that the objects and the background are unchanging.

But it is fair to wonder whether it is possible to generate variations of the 3D scene. Can we control the number of objects, their poses, and the scene background? Can we learn about the 3D nature of things without posed images and without understanding the camera parameters?

By the end of this chapter, you will learn that it is indeed possible to do all these things. Concretely, you should have a better understanding of GIRAFFE, a very novel method for controllable 3D image synthesis. This combines ideas from the fields of image synthesis and implicit 3D representation learning using NeRF-like models. This will become clear as we cover the following topics:

- Understanding GAN-based image synthesis
- Introducing compositional 3D-aware image synthesis
- Generating feature fields
- Mapping feature fields to images
- Exploring controllable scene generation
- Training the GIRAFFE model

Technical requirements

In order to run the example code snippets in this book, ideally, you need to have a computer with a GPU that has around 8 GB of GPU memory. Running code snippets with only CPUs is not impossible but will be extremely slow. The recommended computer configuration is as follows:

- A GPU device – for example, the Nvidia GTX series or the RTX series with at least 8 GB of memory

- Python 3.7+

- Anaconda3

The code snippets for this chapter can be found at https://github.com/PacktPublishing/3D-Deep-Learning-with-Python.

Understanding GAN-based image synthesis

Deep generative models have been shown to produce photorealistic 2D images when trained on a distribution from a particular domain. **Generative Adversarial Networks** (**GANs**) are one of the most widely used frameworks for this purpose. They can synthesize high-quality photorealistic images at resolutions of 1,024 x 1,024 and beyond. For example, they have been used to generate realistic faces:

Figure 7.1: Randomly generated faces as high-quality 2D images using StyleGAN2

GANs can be trained to generate similar-looking images from any data distribution. The same StyleGAN2 model, when trained on a car dataset, can generate high-resolution images of cars:

Figure 7.2: Randomly generated cars as 2D images using StyleGAN2

GANs are based on a game-theoretic scenario where a generator neural network generates an image. However, in order to be successful, it must fool the discriminator into classifying it as a realistic image. This tug of war between the two neural networks (that is, the generator and the discriminator) can lead to a generator that produces photorealistic images. The generator network does this by creating a probability distribution on a multi-dimensional latent space such that the points on that distribution are realistic images from the domain of the training images. In order to generate a novel image, we just need to sample a point on the latent space and let the generator create an image from it:

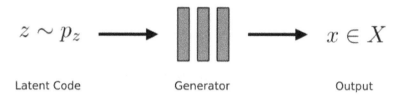

$$z \sim p_z \longrightarrow \text{Generator} \longrightarrow x \in X$$

Latent Code   Generator   Output

Figure 7.3: A canonical GAN

Synthesizing high-resolution photorealistic images is great, but it is not the only desirable property of a generative model. More real-life applications open if the generation process is disentangled and controllable in a simple and predictable manner. More importantly, we need attributes such as object shape, size, and pose to be as disentangled as possible so that we can vary them without changing other attributes in the image.

Existing GAN-based image generation approaches generate 2D images without truly understanding the underlying 3D nature of the image. Therefore, there are no built-in explicit controls for varying attributes such as object position, shape, size, and pose. This results in GANs that have entangled attributes. For simplicity, think about an example of a GAN model that generates realistic faces, where changing the head pose also changes the perceived gender of the generated face. This can happen if the gender and head pose attributes become entangled. This is undesirable for most practical use cases. We need to be able to vary one attribute without affecting any of the others.

In the next section, we are going to look at a high-level overview of a model that can generate 2D images with an implicit understanding of the 3D nature of the underlying scene.

Introducing compositional 3D-aware image synthesis

Our goal is controllable image synthesis. We need control over the number of objects in the image, their position, shape, size, and pose. The GIRAFFE model is one of the first to achieve all these desirable properties while also generating high-resolution photorealistic images. In order to have control over these attributes, the model must have some awareness of the 3D nature of the scene.

Now, let us look at how the GIRAFFE model builds on top of other established ideas to achieve this. It makes use of the following high-level concepts:

- **Learning 3D representation**: A NeRF-like model for learning implicit 3D representation and feature fields. Unlike the standard NeRF model, this model outputs a feature field instead of the color intensity. This NeRF-like model is used to enforce a 3D consistency in the images generated.

- **Compositional operator**: A parameter-free compositional operator to compose feature fields of multiple objects into a single feature field. This will help in creating images with the desired number of objects in them.

- **Neural rendering model**: This uses the composed feature field to create an image. This is a 2D **Convolutional Neural Network** (**CNN**) that upsamples the feature field to create a higher dimensional output image.

- **GAN**: The GIRAFFE model uses the GAN model architecture to generate new scenes. The preceding three components form the generator. The model also consists of a discriminator neural network that distinguishes between fake images and real images. Due to the presence of a NeRF model along with a composition operator, this model will make the image generation process both compositional and 3D aware.

Generating an image is a two-step process:

1. Volume-render a feature field given the camera viewing angle along with some information about the objects you want to render. This object information is some abstract vectors that you will learn about in future sections.

2. Use a neural rendering model to map the feature field to a high-resolution image.

This two-step approach was found to be better at generating high-resolution images as compared to directly generating the RGB values from the NeRF model output. From the previous chapter, we know that a NeRF model is trained on images from the same scene. A trained model can only generate an image from the same scene. This was one of the big limitations of the NeRF model.

In contrast, the GIRAFFE model is trained on images of unposed images from different scenes. A trained model can generate images from the same distribution as what it was trained on. Typically, this model is trained on the same kind of data. That is, the training data distribution comes from a single domain. For example, if we train a model on the *Cars* dataset, we can expect the images generated by this model to be some version of a car. It cannot generate images from a completely unseen distribution such as faces. While this is still a limitation of what the model can do, it is much less limited as compared to the standard NeRF model.

The fundamental concepts implemented in the GIRAFFE model that we have discussed so far are summarized in the following diagram:

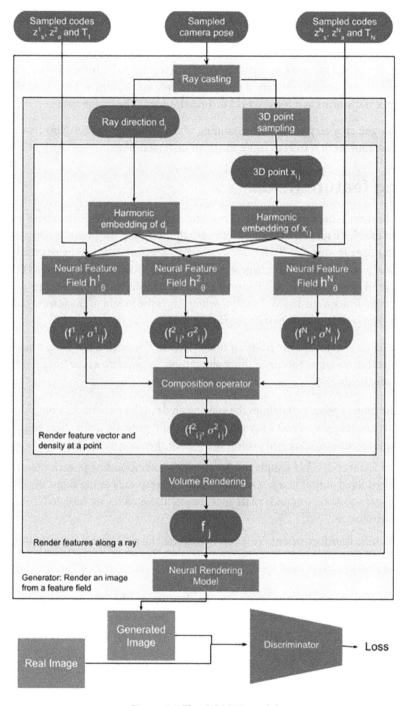

Figure 7.4: The GIRAFFE model

The generator model uses the chosen camera pose and N, the number of objects (including the background), and the corresponding number of shape and appearance codes along with affine transformations to first synthesize feature fields. The individual feature fields corresponding to individual objects are then composed together to form an aggregate feature field. It then volume renders the feature field along the ray using the standard principles of volume rendering. Following this, a neural rendering network transforms this feature field to a pixel value in the image space.

In this section, we gained a very broad understanding of the GIRAFFE model. Now let us zoom into the individual components of it to get a more in-depth understanding.

Generating feature fields

The first step of the scene generation process is generating a feature field. This is analogous to generating an RGB image in the NeRF model. In the NeRF model, the output of the model is a feature field that happens to be an image made up of RGB values. However, a feature field can be any abstract notion of the image. It is a generalization of an image matrix. The difference here is that instead of generating a three-channel RGB image, the GIRAFFE model generates a more abstract image that we refer to as the feature field with dimensions H_v, W_v, and M_f, where H_v is the height of the feature field, W_v is its width, and M_f is the number of channels in the feature field.

For this section, let us assume that we have a trained GIRAFFE model. It has been trained on some predefined dataset that we are not going to think about now. To generate a new image, we need to do the following three things:

1. Specify the camera pose: This defines the viewing angle of the camera. As a preprocessing step, we use this camera pose to cast a ray into the scene and generate a direction vector (dj) along with sampled points (x_{ij}). We will project many such rays into the scene.

2. Sample 2N latent codes: We sample two latent codes corresponding to each object we wish to see in the rendered output image. One latent code corresponds to the shape of the object and the other latent code corresponds to its appearance. These codes are sampled from a standard normal distribution.

3. Specify N affine transformations: This corresponds to the pose of the object in the scene.

The generator part of the model does the following:

*   For each expected object in the scene, use the shape code, the appearance code, the object's pose information (that is, the affine transformation), the viewing direction vector, and a point in the scene (x_{ij}) to generate a feature field (a vector) and a volume density for that point. This is the NeRF model in action.

- Use the compositional operator to compose these feature fields and densities into a single feature field and density value for that point. Here, the compositional operator does the following:

$$\sigma = \sum_{i=1}^{N} \sigma\_i$$

$$f = \frac{1}{\sigma} \sum_{i=1}^{N} \sigma_i * f\_i$$

The volume density at a point can be simply summed up. The feature field is averaged by assigning importance proportional to the volume density of the object at that point. One important benefit of such a simple operator is that it is differentiable. Therefore, it can be introduced inside a neural network since the gradients can flow through this operator during the model training phase.

- We use volume rendering to render a feature field for each ray generated for the input camera pose by aggregating feature field values along the ray. We do this for multiple rays to create a full feature field of dimension H_V x W_V. Here, V is generally a small value. So, we are creating a low-resolution feature field.

> **Feature fields**
>
> A feature field is an abstract notion of an image. They are not RGB values and are typically in low spatial dimensions (such as 16 x 16 or 64 x 64) but high channel dimensions. We need an image that is spatially high dimensional (for example, 512 x 512), but in three channels (RGB). Let us look at a way to do that with a neural network.

Mapping feature fields to images

After we generate a feature field of dimensions H_V x W_V x M_f, we need to map this to an image of dimension H x W x 3. Typically, H_V < H, W_V < W, and M_f > 3. The GIRAFFE model uses the two-stage approach since an ablation analysis showed it to be better than using a single-stage approach to generate the image directly.

The mapping operation is a parametric function that can be learned with data, and using a 2D CNN is best suited for this task since it is a function in the image domain. You can think of this function as an upsampling neural network like a decoder in an auto-encoder. The output of this neural network is the rendered image that we can see, understand, and evaluate. Mathematically, this can be defined as follows:

$$\pi_\theta^{neural} : \mathbb{R}^{H_v \times W_v \times M_f} \rightarrow \mathbb{R}^{H \times W \times 3}$$

This neural network consists of a series of upsampling layers done using n blocks of nearest neighbor upsampling, followed by a 3 x 3 convolution and leaky ReLU. This creates a series of n different spatial resolutions of the feature field. However, in each spatial resolution, the feature field is mapped to a three-channel image of the same spatial resolution via a 3 x 3 convolution. At the same time, images from the previous spatial resolution are upsampled using a non-parametric bilinear upsampling operator and added to the image of the new spatial resolution. This is repeated until we reach the desired spatial resolution of H x W.

The skip connections from the feature field to a similar dimensional image help with a strong gradient flow to the feature fields in each spatial resolution. Intuitively, this ensures that the neural rendering model has a strong understanding of the image in each spatial resolution. Additionally, the skip connections ensure that the final image that is generated is a combination of the image understanding at various resolutions.

This concept becomes very clear with the following diagram of the neural rendering model:

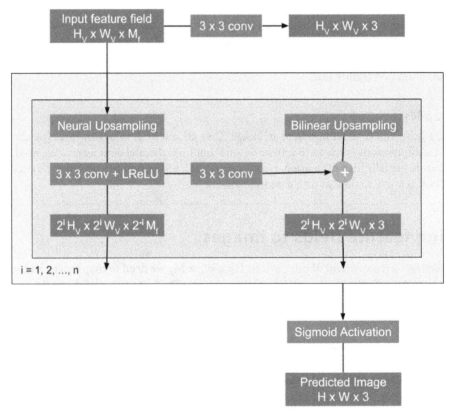

Figure 7.5: Neural rendering model; this is a 2D CNN with a series of nearest neighbor upsampling operators with a parallel mapping to the RGB image domain

The neural rendering model takes the feature field output from the previous stage and generates a high-resolution RGB image. Since the feature field is generated using a NeRF-based generator, it should understand the 3D nature of the scene, the objects in them, and their position, pose, shape, and appearance. And since we use a compositional operator, the feature field also encodes the number of objects in the scene.

In the next section, you will discover how we can control the scene generation process and the control mechanisms we have to achieve it.

Exploring controllable scene generation

To truly appreciate and learn what a computer vision model generates, we need to visualize the outputs of the trained model. Since we are dealing with a generative approach, it is easy to do this by simply visualizing the images generated by the model. In this section, we will explore pre-trained GIRAFFE models and look at how well they can generate controllable scenes. We will use pre-trained checkpoints provided by the creators of the GIRAFFE model. The instructions provided in this section are based on the open source GitHub repository at `https://github.com/autonomousvision/giraffe`.

Create the Anaconda environment called `giraffe` with the following commands:

```
$ cd chap7/giraffe
$ conda env create -f environment.yml
$ conda activate giraffe
```

Once the `conda` environment has been activated, you can start rendering images for various datasets using their corresponding pre-trained checkpoints. The creators of the GIRAFFE model have shared pre-trained models from five different datasets:

- **Cars dataset**: This consists of 136,726 images of 196 classes of cars.

- **CelebA-HQ dataset**: This consists of 30,000 high-resolution face images selected from the original *CelebA* dataset.

- **LSUN Church dataset**: This consists of about 126,227 images of churches.

- **CLEVR dataset**: This is a dataset primarily used for visual question-answering research. It consists of 54,336 images of objects of different sizes, shapes, and positions.

- **Flickr-Faces-HQ dataset**: This consists of 70,000 high-quality images of faces obtained from Flickr.

We will explore the model outputs on two different datasets just to get an understanding of them.

Exploring controllable car generation

In this subsection, we are going to explore a model trained on the *Cars* dataset. The appearance and shape code provided to the model will generate cars since that is what the model is trained on. You can run the following command to generate image samples:

```
$ python render.py configs/256res/cars_256_pretrained.yaml
```

Here, the `config` file specifies the path to the output folder where the generated images are stored. The `render.py` script will automatically download the GIRAFFE model checkpoints and use them to render images. The output images are stored in `out/cars256_pretrained/rendering`. This folder will have the following subfolders:

```
- out
  - cars256_pretrained
    - rendering
      - interpolate_app
      - interpolate_shape
      - translation_object_depth
      - interpolate_bg_app
      - rotation_object
      - translation_object_horizontal
```

Each of these folders contains images obtained when we change specific inputs of the GIRAFFE model. For example, take a look at the following:

- `interpolate_app`: This is a set of images to demonstrate what happens when we slowly vary the object appearance code.

- `interpolate_bg_app`: This demonstrates what happens when we vary the background appearance code.

- `interpolate_shape`: This demonstrates what happens when we vary the shape code of the object.

- `translation_object_depth`: This demonstrates what happens when we change the object depth. This is part of the affine transformation matrix code that is part of the input.

- `translation_object_horizontal`: This demonstrates what happens when we want to move the object sideways in the image. This is part of the affine transformation matrix code that is part of the input.

- `rotation_object`: This demonstrates what happens when we want to change the object pose. This is part of the affine transformation matrix code that is part of the input.

Let us look at the images inside the `rotation_object` folder and analyze them:

Figure 7.6: The Rotation object model images

Images in each row were obtained by, first, choosing an appearance and shape code and varying the affine transformation matrix to just rotate the object. The horizontal and depth translation parts of the affine transformation code were kept fixed. The background object code, appearance, and shape code of the object were also kept fixed. Different rows were obtained by using different appearance and shape code. Here are some observations:

- The background for all the images does not change across images for the same object. This suggests that we have successfully disentangled the background for the remaining parts of the image.

- Color, reflection, and shadows: As the object is rotated, the image color and reflection are fairly consistent as expected of a physical object rotation. This is typical because of the usage of NeRF-like model architecture.

- Left-right consistency: The left and right views of a car are consistent.

- There are some unnatural artifacts such as blurry object edges and smudged backgrounds. High-frequency variations in the image are not very well captured by the GIRAFFE model.

You can now explore other folders to understand the model's consistency and quality of the generated image when the object is translated or when the background is varied.

Exploring controllable face generation

In this subsection, we are going to explore a model trained on the *CelebA-HQ* dataset. The appearance and shape codes provided to the model will generate faces since that is what the model is trained on. You can run the following command to generate image samples:

```
$ python render.py configs/256res/celebahq_256_pretrained.yaml
```

The `config` file specifies the path to the output folder where the generated images are stored. The output images are stored in `out/celebahq_256_pretrained /rendering`. This folder will have the following subfolders:

```
- out
  - celebahq_256_pretrained
    - rendering
      - interpolate_app
      - interpolate_shape
      - rotation_object
```

Let us look at images inside the `interpolate_app` folder and analyze them:

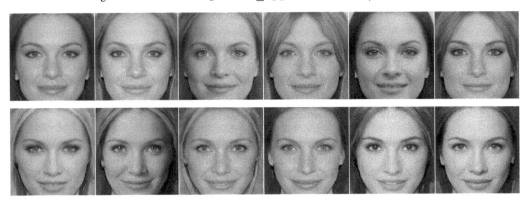

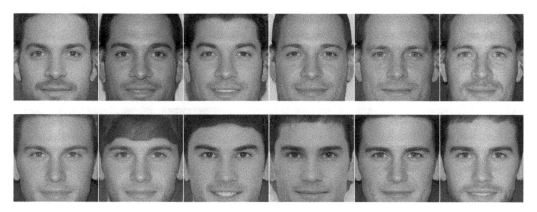

Figure 7.7: The interpolate app images

Images in each row were obtained by, first, choosing a shape code and varying the appearance code to just change the appearance of the face. The affine transformation matrix code was kept fixed too. Different rows were obtained by using different shape code. Here are some observations:

- The shape of the generated face is largely fixed across a single row of faces. This suggests that the shape code is robust to changes in appearance code.

- The appearance of the face (features such as skin tone, skin shine, hair color, eyebrow color, eye color, lip expression, and nose shape) changes as the appearance code is changed. This suggests that the appearance code encodes facial appearance features.

- The shape code encodes the perceived gender of the face. This largely makes sense since there is a large perceived variation between the facial shape of male and female images in the training dataset.

Let us look at images inside the `interpolate_shape` folder and analyze them:

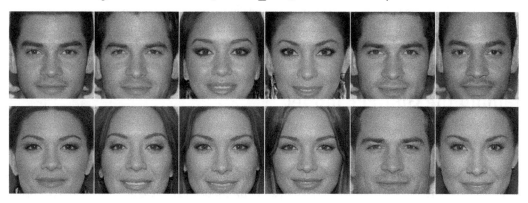

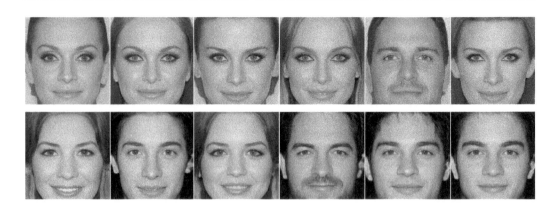

Figure 7.8: The interpolate shape images

Images in each row were obtained by, first, choosing an appearance code and varying the shape code to just change the shape of the face. The affine transformation matrix code was kept fixed too. Different rows were obtained by using different appearance code. Here are some observations:

- The appearance of the face (features such as skin tone, skin shine, hair color, eyebrow color, eye color, lip expression, and nose shape) is largely the same as the shape code is changed. This suggests that the appearance code is robust to changes in facial shape features.

- The shape of the generated face changes as the shape code is varied. This suggests that the shape code is correctly encoding the shape features of the face.

- The shape code encodes the perceived gender of the face. This largely makes sense since there is a large perceived variation between the facial shape of male and female images in the training dataset.

In this section, we explored controllable 3D scene generation using the GIRAFFE model. We generated cars using a model trained on the *Cars* dataset. Additionally, we generated faces using a model trained on the *CelebA-HQ* dataset. In each of these cases, we saw that the input parameters of the model are very well disentangled. We used a pre-trained model provided by the creators of the GIRAFFE model. In the next section, we will learn more about how to train such a model on a new dataset.

Training the GIRAFFE model

So far in this chapter, we have understood how a trained GIRAFFE model works. We have understood the different components that make up the generator part of the model.

But to train the model, there is another part that we have not looked at so far, namely, the discriminator. Like in any other GAN model, this discriminator part of the model is not used during image synthesis, but it is a vital component for training the model. In this chapter, we will investigate it in more detail and gain an understanding of the loss function used. We will train a new model from scratch using the training module provided by the authors of GIRAFFE.

The generator takes as input the various latent code corresponding to object rotation, background rotation, camera elevation, horizontal and depth translation, and object size. This is used to first generate a feature field and then map it to RGB pixels using a neural rendering module. This is the generator. The discriminator is fed with two images: one is the real image from the training dataset and the other is the image generated by the generator. The goal of the discriminator is to classify the real image as real and the generated image as fake. This is the GAN objective.

> **Important note**
>
> The training dataset is unlabeled. There is no annotation for the object pose parameters, depth, or position in the image. However, for each dataset, we roughly know the parameters such as object rotation rate, background rotation range, camera elevation range, horizontal translation, depth translation range, and the object scale range. During training, the inputs are randomly sampled from the range of values assuming a uniform distribution within the range.

The discriminator is a 2D CNN that takes as input an image and outputs confidence scores for real and fake images.

Frechet Inception Distance

In order to evaluate the quality of generated images, we use the **Frechet Inception Distance (FID)**. This is a measure of the distance between features extracted from real and generated images. This is not a metric on a single image. Rather, it is a statistic on the entire population of the images. Here is how we calculate the FID score:

1. First, we make use of the InceptionV3 model (a popular deep learning backbone used in many real-world applications) to extract a feature vector from the image. Typically, this is the last layer of the model before the classification layer. This feature vector summarizes the image in a low-dimensional space.

2. We extract feature vectors for the entire collection of real and generated images.

3. We calculate the mean and the covariance of these feature vectors separately for the collection of real and generated images.

4. The mean and covariance statistics are used in a distance formula to derive a distance metric.

Training the model

Let us look at how can initiate model training on the *Cars* dataset:

```
python train.py .yaml configs/256res/celebahq_256.yaml
```

The training parameters can be understood by looking at the configuration file, `configs/256res/celebahq_256.yaml`:

- **Data**: This section of the config file specifies the path to the training dataset to use:

```
data:
  path: data/comprehensive_cars/images/*.jpg
  fid_file: data/comprehensive_cars/fid_files/
comprehensiveCars_256.npz
  random_crop: True
  img_size: 256
```

- **Model**: This specifies the modeling parameters:

```
model:
  background_generator_kwargs:
    rgb_out_dim: 256
  bounding_box_generator_kwargs:
    scale_range_min: [0.2, 0.16, 0.16]
    scale_range_max: [0.25, 0.2, 0.2]
    translation_range_min: [-0.22, -0.12, 0.]
    translation_range_max: [0.22, 0.12, 0.]
  generator_kwargs:
    range_v: [0.41667, 0.5]
    fov: 10
  neural_renderer_kwargs:
    input_dim: 256
    n_feat: 256
  decoder_kwargs:
    rgb_out_dim: 256
```

- **Training**: This specifies the training parameters such as output d
- Directory path and learning rate, among other things:

```
training:
  out_dir:   out/cars256
  learning_rate: 0.00025
```

> **Important note**
>
> Training the model is a computationally intensive task. It would most likely take anywhere between 1 and 4 days to fully train the model on a single GPU, depending on the GPU device used.

Summary

In this chapter, you explored controllable 3D-aware image synthesis using the GIRAFFE model. This model borrows concepts from NeRF, GANs, and 2D CNNs to create 3D scenes that are controllable. First, we had a refresher on GANs. Then, we dove deeper into the GIRAFFE model, how feature fields are generated, and how those feature fields are then transformed into RGB images. We then explored the outputs of this model and understood its properties and limitations. Finally, we briefly touched on how to train this model.

In the next chapter, we are going to explore a relatively new technique used to generate realistic human bodies in three dimensions called the SMPL model. Notably, the SMPL model is one of the small numbers of models that do not use deep neural networks. Instead, it uses more classical statistical techniques such as principal component analysis to achieve its objectives. You will learn the importance of good mathematical problem formulation in building models that use classical techniques.

8

Modeling the Human Body in 3D

In the previous chapters, we explored ideas for modeling a 3D scene and the objects in them. Most of the objects we modeled were static and unchanging, but many applications of computer vision in real life center around humans in their natural habitat. We want to model their interactions with other humans and objects in the scene.

There are several applications for this. Snapchat filters, FaceRig, virtual try-on, and motion capture technology in Hollywood all benefit from accurate 3D body modeling. Consider, for example, an automated checkout technology. Here, a retail store is equipped with several depth-sensing cameras. They might want to detect whenever a person retrieves an object and modify their checkout basket accordingly. Such an application and many more will require us to accurately model the human body.

Human pose estimation is a cornerstone problem of human body modeling. Such a model can predict the location of joints such as shoulders, hips, and elbows to create a skeleton of the person in an image. They are then used for several downstream applications such as action recognition and human-object interaction. However, modeling a human body as a set of joints has its limitations:

- Human joints are not visible and never interact with the physical world. So, we cannot rely on them to accurately model human-object interactions.

- Joints do not model the topology, volume, and surface of the body. For certain applications, such as modeling how clothing fits, joints alone are not useful.

We can come to an agreement that human pose models are functional for some applications but certainly not realistic. How can we realistically model the human body? Will that address these limitations? What other applications can this unlock? We answer these questions in this chapter. Concretely, we will cover the following topics:

- Formulating the 3D modeling problem

- Understanding the Linear Blend Skinning technique

- Understanding the SMPL model

- Using the SMPL model

- Estimating 3D human pose and shape using SMPLify

- Exploring SMPLify

Technical requirements

The computation requirements for the code in this chapter are pretty low. However, running this in a Linux environment is recommended since it has better support for certain libraries. However, it is not impossible to run this in other environments. In the coding sections, we describe in detail how to set up the environment to successfully run the code. We will need the following technical requirements for this chapter:

- Python 2.7

- Libraries such as opendr, matplotlib, opencv, and numpy.

The code snippets for this chapter can be found at `https://github.com/PacktPublishing/3D-Deep-Learning-with-Python`.

Formulating the 3D modeling problem

"All models are wrong, but some are useful" is a popular aphorism in statistics. It suggests that it is often hard to mathematically model all the tiny details of a problem. A model will always be an approximation of reality, but some models are more accurate and, therefore, more useful than others.

In the field of machine learning, modeling a problem generally involves the following two components:

- Mathematically formulating the problem

- Building algorithms to solve that problem under the constraints and boundaries of that formulation

Good algorithms used on badly formulated problems often result in sub-optimal models. However, less powerful algorithms applied to a well-formulated model can sometimes result in great solutions. This insight is especially true for building 3D human body models.

The goal of this modeling problem is to create realistic animated human bodies. More importantly, this should represent realistic body shapes and must deform naturally according to changes in body pose and capture soft tissue motions. Modeling the human body in 3D is a hard challenge. The human body has a mass of bones, organs, skin, muscles, and water and they interact with each other in complex ways. To exactly model the human body, we need to model the behavior of all these individual components and their interactions with each other. This is a hard challenge, and for some practical applications, this level of exactness is unnecessary. In this chapter, we will model the human body's surface and shape in 3D as a proxy for modeling the entire human body. We do not need the model to be exact; we just need it to have a realistic external appearance. This makes the problem more approachable.

Defining a good representation

The goal is to represent the human body accurately with a low-dimensional representation. Joint models are low-dimensional representations (typically 17 to 25 points in 3D space) but do not carry a lot of information about the shape and texture of the person. On another end, we can consider the voxel grid representation. This can model the 3D body shape and texture, but it is extremely highly dimensional and does not naturally lend itself to modeling body dynamics due to pose changes.

Therefore, we need a representation that can jointly represent body joints and surfaces, which contains information about body volume. There are several candidate representations for surfaces; one such representation is a mesh of vertices. The **Skinned Multi-Person Linear** (**SMPL**) model uses this representation. Once specified, this mesh of vertices will describe the 3D shape of a human body.

Because there is a lot of history to this problem, we will find that many artists in the character animation industry have worked on building good body meshes. The SMPL model uses such expert insights to build a good initial template of a body mesh. This is an important first step because certain parts of the body have high-frequency variations (such as the face and hands). Such high-frequency variations need more densely packed points to describe them, but body parts with lower frequency variations (such as thighs) need less dense points to accurately describe them. Such a hand-crafted initial mesh will help bring down the dimensionality of the problem while keeping the necessary information to accurately model it. This mesh in the SMPL model is gender-neutral, but you can build variations for men and women separately.

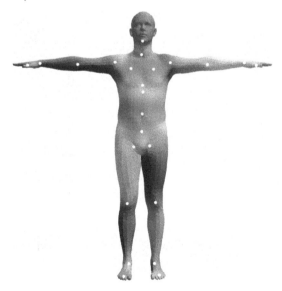

Figure 8.1 – The SMPL model template mesh in the resting pose

More concretely, the initial template mesh consists of 6,890 points in 3D space to represent the human body surface. When this is vectorized, this template mesh has a vector length of 6,890 x 3 = 20,670. Any human body can be obtained by distorting this template mesh vector to fit the body surface.

It sounds like a remarkably simple concept on paper, but the number of configurations of a 20,670-dimensional vector is extremely high. The set of configurations that represents a real human body is an extremely tiny subset of all the possibilities. The problem then becomes defining a method to obtain a plausible configuration that represents a real human body.

Before we understand how the SMPL model is designed, we need to learn about skinning models. In the next section, we will look at one of the simplest skinning techniques: the Linear Blend Skinning technique. This is important because the SMPL model is built on top of this technique.

Understanding the Linear Blend Skinning technique

Once we have a good representation of the 3D human body, we want to model how it looks in different poses. This is particularly important for character animation. The idea is that **skinning** involves enveloping an underlying skeleton with a skin (a surface) that conveys the appearance of the object being animated. This is a term used in the animation industry. Typically, this representation takes the form of vertices, which are then used to define connected polygons to form the surface.

The Linear Blend Skinning model is used to take a skin in the resting pose and transform it into a skin in any arbitrary pose using a simple linear model. This is so efficient to render that many game engines support this technique, and it is also used to render game characters in real time.

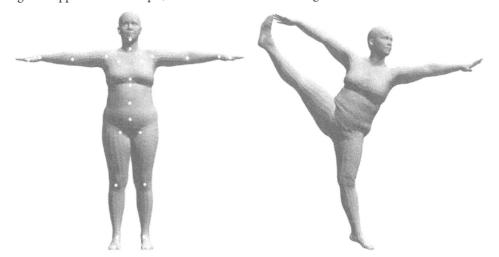

Figure 8.2 – Initial blend shape (left) and deformed mesh generated with blend skinning (right)

Let us now understand what this technique involves. This technique is a model that uses the following parameters:

- A template mesh, T, with N vertices. In this case, N = 6,890.

- We have the K joint locations represented by the vector J. These joints correspond to joints in the human body (such as shoulders, wrists, and ankles). There are 23 of these joints (K = 23).

- Blend weights, W. This is typically a matrix of size N x K that captures the relationship between the N surface vertices and the K joints of the body.

- The pose parameters, Θ. These are the rotation parameters for each of the K joints. There are 3K of these parameters. In this case, we have 72 of them. 69 of these parameters correspond to 23 joints and 3 correspond to the overall body rotation.

The skinning function takes the resting pose mesh, the joint locations, the blend weights, and the pose parameters as input and produces the output vertices:

$$W(T, J, W, \vec{\theta}) \rightarrow vertices$$

In Linear Blend Skinning, the function takes the form of a simple linear function of the transformed template vertices as described in the following equation:

$$\vec{t_i} = \sum_{k=1}^{K} w_{k,i} \, G_k'(\vec{\theta}, J)$$

The meaning of these terms is the following:

- t_i represents the vertices in the original mesh in the resting pose.

- $G(\Theta, J)$ is the matrix that transforms the joint k from the resting pose to the target pose.

- w_k, i are elements of the blend weights, W. They represent the amount of influence the joint k has on the vertex i.

While this is an easy-to-use linear model and is very well used in the animation industry, it does not explicitly preserve volume. Therefore, transformations can look unnatural.

In order to fix this problem, artists tweak the template mesh so that when the skinning model is applied, the outcome looks natural and realistic. Such linear deformations applied to the template mesh to obtain realistic-looking transformed mesh are called blend shapes. These blend shapes are artist-designed for all of the different poses the animated character can have. This is a very time-consuming process.

As we will see later, the SMPL model automatically calculates the blend shapes before applying the skinning model to them. In the next section, you will learn about how the SMPL model creates such pose-dependent blend shapes and how data is used to guide it.

Understanding the SMPL model

As the acronym of SMPL suggests, this is a learned linear model trained on data from thousands of people. This model is built upon concepts from the Linear Blend Skinning model. It is an unsupervised and generative model that generates a 20,670-dimensional vector using the provided input parameters that we can control. This model calculates the blend shapes required to produce the correct deformations for varying input parameters. We need these input parameters to have the following important properties:

- It should correspond to a real tangible attribute of the human body.

- The features must be low-dimensional in nature. This will enable us to easily control the generative process.

- The features must be disentangled and controllable in a predictable manner. That is, varying one parameter should not change the output characteristics attributed to other parameters.

Keeping these requirements in mind, the creators of the SMPL model came up with the two most important input attributes: some notion of body identity and body pose. The SMPL model decomposes the final 3D body mesh into an identity-based shape and pose-based shape (identity-based shape is also referred to as shape-based shape because the body shape is tied to a person's identity). This gives the model the desired property of feature disentanglement. There are some other important factors such as breathing and soft tissue dynamics (when the body is in motion) that we do not explain in this chapter but are part of the SMPL model.

Most importantly, the SMPL model is an additive model of deformations. That is, the desired output body shape vector is obtained by adding deformations to the original template body vector. This additive property makes this model very intuitive to understand and optimize.

Defining the SMPL model

The SMPL model builds on top of the standard skinning models. It makes the following changes to it:

- Rather than using the standard resting pose template, it uses a template mesh that is a function of the body shape and poses

- Joint locations are a function of the body shape

The function specified by the SMPL model takes the following form:

$$M(\vec{\beta}, \vec{\theta}) = W(T_p(\vec{\beta}, \vec{\theta})J(\vec{\beta}), \vec{\theta}, W)$$

The following is the meaning of the terms in the preceding definitions:

- β is a vector representing the identity (also called the shape) of the body. We will later learn more about what it represents.

- Θ is the pose parameter corresponding to the target pose.

- W is the blend weight from the Linear Blend Skinning model.

This function looks very similar to the Linear Blend Skinning model. In this function, the template mesh is a function of shape and pose parameters, and the joint's location is a function of shape parameters. This is not the case in the Linear Blend Skinning model.

Shape and pose-dependent template mesh

The redefined template mesh is an additive linear deformation of the standard template mesh:

$$T_p(\vec{\beta}, \vec{\theta}) = \overline{T} + B_S(\vec{\beta}) + B_P(\vec{\theta})$$

Here, we see the following:

- $B_S(\vec{\beta})$ is an additive deformation from the body shape parameters β. It is a learned deformation modeled as the first few principal components of the shape displacements. These principal components are obtained from the training data involving different people in the same resting pose.

- $B_P(\vec{\theta})$ is an additive pose deformation term. This is parametrized by Θ. This is also a linear function learned from a multi-pose dataset of people in different poses.

Shape-dependent joints

Since joint locations depend on the body shape, they are redefined as a function of body shape. The SMPL model defines this in the following manner:

$$j(\vec{\beta}; J, \overline{T}, S) = J(\overline{T} + B_S(\vec{\beta}; S))$$

Here, $B_S(\vec{\beta})$ is the additive deformation from the body shape parameters β, and J is a matrix that transforms the rest template vertices to the rest template poses. The parameters of J are also learned from data.

Using the SMPL model

Now that you have a high-level understanding of the SMPL model, we will look at how to use it to create 3D models of humans. In this section, we will start with a few basic functions; this will help you explore the SMPL model. We will load the SMPL model, and edit the shape and pose parameters to create a new 3D body. We will then save this as an object file and visualize it.

This code was originally created by the authors of SMPL for python2. Therefore, we need to create a separate python2 environment. The following are the instructions for this:

```
cd chap8
conda create -n python2 python=2.7 anaconda
```

```
source activate python2
pip install -r requirements.txt
```

This creates and activates the Python 2.7 conda environment and installs the required modules. Python 2.7 is being deprecated, so you might see warning messages when you try to use it. In order to create a 3D human body with random shape and pose parameters, run the following command.

```
$ python render_smpl.py
```

This will pop up a window that shows the rendering of a human body in 3D. Our output will likely be different since render_smpl.py creates a human body with random pose and shape parameters.

Figure 8.3 – An example rendering of the hello_smpl.obj created by explore_smpl.py

Now that we have run the code and obtained a visual output, let us explore what is happening in the render_smpl.py file:

1. Import all of the required modules:

    ```
    import cv2
    import numpy as np
    from opendr.renderer import ColoredRenderer
    from opendr.lighting import LambertianPointLight
    from opendr.camera import ProjectPoints
    from smpl.serialization import load_model
    ```

2. Load the model weights of the basic SMPL model. Here, we load the neural body model:

    ```
    m = load_model('../smplify/code/models/basicModel_
    neutral_lbs_10_207_0_v1.0.0.pkl')
    ```

3. Next, we assign random pose and shape parameters. The following pose and shape parameters dictate how the 3D body mesh looks in the end:

    ```
    m.pose[:] = np.random.rand(m.pose.size) * .2
    m.betas[:] = np.random.rand(m.betas.size) * .03
    m.pose[0] = np.pi
    ```

4. We now create a renderer and assign attributes to it, and we construct the light source. By default, we use the OpenDR renderer, but you can switch this to use the PyTorch3D renderer and light source. Before doing that, make sure to address any Python incompatibility issues.

    ```
    rn = ColoredRenderer()
    w, h = (640, 480)
    rn.camera = ProjectPoints(v=m, rt=np.zeros(3), t=np.
    array([0, 0, 2.]), f=np.array([w,w])/2., c=np.
    array([w,h])/2., k=np.zeros(5))
    rn.frustum = {'near': 1., 'far': 10., 'width': w,
    'height': h}
    rn.set(v=m, f=m.f, bgcolor=np.zeros(3))
    rn.vc = LambertianPointLight(f=m.f, v=rn.v, num_
    verts=len(m), light_pos=np.array([-1000,-1000,-2000]),
    vc=np.ones_like(m)*.9, light_color=np.array([1., 1.,
    1.]))
    ```

5. We can now render the mesh and display it in an OpenCV window:

    ```
    cv2.imshow('render_SMPL', rn.r)
    cv2.waitKey(0)
    cv2.destroyAllWindows()
    ```

We have now used the SMPL model to generate a random 3D human body. In reality, we might be interested in generating 3D shapes that are more controllable. We will look at how to do this in the next section.

Estimating 3D human pose and shape using SMPLify

In the previous section, you explored the SMPL model and used it to generate a 3D human body with a random shape and pose. It is natural to wonder whether it is possible to use the SMPL model to fit a 3D human body onto a person in a 2D image. This has multiple practical applications, such as understanding human actions or creating animations from 2D videos. This is indeed possible, and in this chapter, we are going to explore this idea in more detail.

Imagine that you are given a single RGB image of a person without any information about body pose, camera parameters, or shape parameters. Our goal is to deduce the 3D shape and pose from just this single image. Estimating the 3D shape from a 2D image is not always error-free. It is a challenging problem because of the complexity of the human body, articulation, occlusion, clothing, lighting, and the inherent ambiguity in inferring 3D from 2D (because multiple 3D poses can have the same 2D pose when projected). We also need an automatic way of estimating this without much manual intervention. It also needs to work on complex poses in natural images with a variety of backgrounds, lighting conditions, and camera parameters.

One of the best methods of doing this was invented by researchers from the Max Planck Institute of Intelligent Systems (where the SMPL model was invented), Microsoft, the University of Maryland, and the University of Tübingen. This approach is called SMPLify. Let us explore this approach in more detail.

The SMPLify approach consists of the following two stages:

1. Automatically detect 2D joints using established pose detection models such as OpenPose or DeepCut. Any 2D joint detectors can be used in their place as long as they are predicting the same joints.

2. Use the SMPL model to generate the 3D shape. Directly optimize the parameters of the SMPL model so that the model joints of the SMPL model project to the 2D joints predicted in the previous stage.

We know that SMPL captures shapes from just the joints. With the SMPL model, we can therefore capture information about body shape just from the joints. In the SMPL model, the body shape parameters are characterized by β. They are the coefficients of the principal components in the PCA shape model. The pose is parametrized by the relative rotation and theta of the 23 joints in the kinematic tree. We need to fit these parameters, β and theta, so that we minimize an objective function.

Defining the optimization objective function

Any objective function must capture our intention to minimize some notion of error. The more accurate this error calculation is, the more accurate the output of the optimization step will be. We will first look at the entire objective function, then look at each of the individual components of that function and explain why each of them is necessary:

$$E_J(\beta, \theta; K, J_{est}) + \lambda_\theta E_\theta(\theta) + \lambda_a E_a(\theta) + \lambda_{sp} E_{sp}(\theta; \beta) + \lambda_\beta E_\beta(\beta)$$

- We want to minimize this objective function by optimizing parameters β and Θ. It consists of four terms and corresponding coefficients, λ_θ, λ_a, λ_{sp}, and λ_β, which are hyperparameters of the optimization process. The following is what each of the individual terms means:

  - $E_J(\beta, \theta; K, J_{est}) = \sum_{joint\ i} w_i \rho(\pi_K(R_\theta(J((\beta)_i))) - J_{est,i})$ is the joint-based term that penalizes the distance between the 2D projected joint of the SMPL model and the predicted joint location from the 2D joint detector (such as DeepCut or OpenPose). w_i is the confidence score of each of the joints provided by the 2D joint detection model. When a joint is occluded, the confidence score for that joint will be low. Naturally, we should not place a lot of importance on such occluded joints.

  - $E_a\theta = \sum_i \exp(\theta_i)$ is the pose that penalizes large angles between joints. For example, it ensures that elbows and knees do not bend unnaturally.

  - $E_a a$ is a Gaussian mixture model fit on natural poses obtained from a very large dataset. This dataset is called the CMU Graphics Lab Motion Capture Database, consisting of nearly one million data points. This data-driven term in the optimization function ensures that the pose parameters are close to what we observe in reality.

1. $E_{sp}(\theta; \beta)$ is the self-penetration error. When the authors optimized the objective function without this error term, they saw unnatural self-penetrations, such as elbows and hands twisted and penetrating through the stomach. This is physically impossible. However, after adding this error term, they found naturally qualitative results. This error term consists of body parts that are approximated as a set of spheres. They define incompatible spheres and penalize the intersection of these incompatible spheres.

2. $E_\beta(\beta) = \beta^T \sum_{\beta}^{-1} \beta$ is the shape obtained from the SMPL model. Note here that the principal component matrix is part of the SMPL model, which was obtained by training on the SMPL training dataset.

In summary, the objective function consists of five components that, together, ensure that the solution to this objective function is a set of pose and shape parameters (theta and beta) that ensure that the 2D join projection distances are minimized while simultaneously ensuring that there are no large joint angles, no unnatural self-penetrations, and that the pose and shape parameters adhere to a prior distribution we see in a large dataset consisting of natural body poses and shapes.

Exploring SMPLify

Now that we have a broad overview of how to estimate the 3D body shape of a person in a 2D RGB image, let us get a hands-on experience with code. Concretely, we are going to fit a 3D body shape onto two 2D images from the **Leeds Sports Pose** (**LSP**) dataset. This dataset contains 2,000 pose-annotated images of mostly sportspeople gathered from Flickr. We will first run through the code and generate these fitted body shapes before we dig deeper into the code. All the code used in this section was adapted from the implementation of the paper titled *Keep it SMPL: Automatic Estimation* *of 3D Human Pose and Shape from a Single Image.* We have only adapted it in a way that helps you, the learner, to quickly run the code and visualize the outputs yourself.

This code was originally created by the authors of SMPLify for `python2`. Therefore, we need to use the same `python2` environment we used while exploring the SMPL model. Before we run any code, let us quickly get an overview of how the code is structured:

```
chap8
  -- smplify
    -- code
      -- fit3d_utils.py
      -- run_fit3d.py
      -- render_model.py
      -- lib
      -- models
    -- images
    -- results
```

Running the code

The main file you will be directly interacting with is `run_fir3d.py`. The folder named `images` will have some example images from the LSP dataset. However, before we run the code, make sure that `PYTHONPATH` is set correctly. This should point to the location of the `chap8` folder. You can run the following code for it:

```
export PYTHONPATH=$PYTHONPATH:<user-specific-path>/3D-Deep-
Learning-with-Python/chap8/
```

Now, go to the right folder:

```
cd smplify/code
```

You can now run the following command to fit a 3D body onto images in the `images` folder:

```
python run_fit3d.py --base_dir ../ --out_dir .
```

This run will not use any interpenetration error since it will be faster to go through the optimization iterations. In the end, we will fit a body-neutral shape. You will be able to visualize the projected pose of the 3D body as it fits the person in the picture. Once the optimization is complete, you will see the following two images:

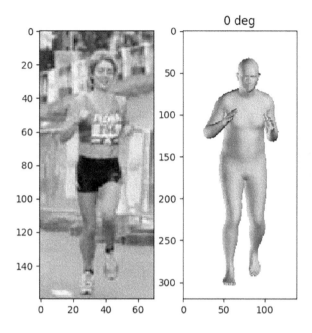

Figure 8.4 – Image in the LSP dataset of a person running (left)
and the 3D body shape fitting this image (right)

Another output is as follows:

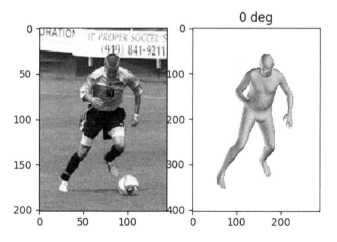

Figure 8.5 – Image in the LSP dataset of a soccer player in action
(left) and the 3D body shape fitting this image (right)

Exploring the code

Now that you have run the code to fit humans in 2D images, let us look at the code in more detail to understand some of the main components needed to achieve this. You will find all the components in `run_fit3d.py`. You need to perform the following steps:

1. Let us first import all of the modules we will need:

```
from os.path import join, exists, abspath, dirname
from os import makedirs
import cPickle as pickle
from glob import glob

import cv2
import numpy as np
import matplotlib.pyplot as plt
import argparse

from smpl.serialization import import load_model
from smplify.code.fit3d_utils import run_single_fit
```

2. Let us now define where our SMPL model is located. This is done through the following:

```
MODEL_DIR = join(abspath(dirname(__file__)), 'models')
MODEL_NEUTRAL_PATH = join(
    MODEL_DIR, 'basicModel_neutral_lbs_10_207_0_v1.0.0.pkl')
```

3. Let us set some parameters required for the optimization method and define the directories where our images and results are located. The results folder will have joint estimates for all the images in the dataset. `viz` is set to `True` to enable visualization. We are using an SMPL model with 10 parameters (that is, it uses 10 principal components to model the body shape). `flength` refers to the focal length of the camera; this is kept fixed during optimization. `pix_thsh` refers to the threshold (in pixels). If the distance between shoulder joints in 2D is lower than `pix_thsh`, the body orientation is ambiguous. This could happen when a person is standing perpendicular to the camera. As a consequence, it is hard to say whether they are facing left or right. So, a fit is run on both the estimated one and its flip:

```
viz = True
n_betas = 10
flength = 5000.0
pix_thsh = 25.0
```

```
img_dir = join(abspath(base_dir), 'images/lsp')
data_dir = join(abspath(base_dir), 'results/lsp')
if not exists(out_dir):
    makedirs(out_dir)
```

4. We should then load this gender-neutral SMPL model into memory:

```
model = load_model(MODEL_NEUTRAL_PATH)
```

5. We then need to load the joint estimates for the images in the LSP dataset. The LSP dataset itself contains joint estimates and corresponding joint confidence scores for all the images in the dataset. We are going to just use that directly. You can also provide your own joint estimates or use good joint estimators, such as OpenPose or DeepCut, to get the joint estimates:

```
est = np.load(join(data_dir, 'est_joints.npz'))['est_
joints']
```

6. Next, we need to load images in the dataset and get the corresponding joint estimates and confidence scores:

```
img_paths = sorted(glob(join(img_dir, '*[0-9].jpg')))
for ind, img_path in enumerate(img_paths):
    img = cv2.imread(img_path)
    joints = est[:2, :, ind].T
    conf = est[2, :, ind]
```

7. For each of the images in the dataset, use the run_single_fit function to fit the parameters beta and theta. The following function returns these parameters after running the optimization on an objective function similar to the SMPLify objective function we discussed in the previous section:

```
params, vis = run_single_fit(img, joints, conf, model,
regs=sph_regs, n_betas=n_betas, flength=flength, pix_
thsh=pix_thsh, scale_factor=2, viz=viz, do_degrees=do_
degrees)
```

While the objective function is being optimized, this function creates a matplotlib window where the green circles are the 2D joint estimates from a 2D joint detection model (which are provided to you). The red circles are the projected joints of the SMPL 3D model that is being fitted onto the 2D image:

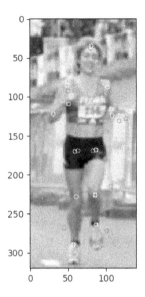

Figure 8.6 – Visualization of the provided 2D joints (green) and the projected
joints (red) of the SMPL model being fit to the 2D image

8. Next, we want to visualize the fitted 3D human body alongside the 2D RGB image. We use matplotlib for this. The following opens up an interactive window where you can save images to disk:

```
if viz:
    import matplotlib.pyplot as plt
    plt.ion()
    plt.show()
    plt.subplot(121)
    plt.imshow(img[:, :, ::-1])
    for di, deg in enumerate(do_degrees):
        plt.subplot(122)
        plt.cla()
        plt.imshow(vis[di])
        plt.draw()
        plt.title('%d deg' % deg)
        plt.pause(1)
        raw_input('Press any key to continue...')
```

9. We then want to save these parameters and visualization to disk with the following code:

```
with open(out_path, 'w') as outf:
    pickle.dump(params, outf)
if do_degrees is not None:
    cv2.imwrite(out_path.replace('.pkl', '.png'),
vis[0])
```

In the preceding code, the most important function is `run_single_fit`. You can explore this function in more detail in `smplify.code.fit3d_utils.py`.

It is important to note here that the accuracy of the fitted 3D body is dependent on the accuracy of the 2D joints. Since the 2D joints are predicted using a joint detection model (such as OpenPose or DeepCut), the accuracy of such joint prediction models becomes very important and relevant to this problem. Estimating 2D joints is especially error-prone in the following scenarios:

- Joints that are not completely visible are hard to predict. This could happen due to a variety of reasons including self-occlusion, occlusion by other objects, unusual clothing, and so on.

- It is easy to confuse between left and right joints (for example, left wrist versus right wrist). This is especially true when the person is facing the camera sideways.

- Detecting joints in unusual poses is hard if the model is not trained with those poses. This depends on the diversity in the dataset used to train the joint detector.

More broadly, a system consisting of multiple machine learning models interacting with each other sequentially (that is, when the output of one model becomes the input of another model) will suffer from cascading errors. Small errors in one component will result in large errors in outputs from downstream components. Such a problem is typically solved by training a system end to end. However, this strategy cannot be used here at the moment since there is no ground-truth data in the research community that directly maps a 2D input image to a 3D model.

Summary

In this chapter, we got an overview of the mathematical formulation of modeling human bodies in 3D. We understood the power of good representation and used simple methods such as Linear Blend Skinning on a powerful representation to obtain realistic outputs. We then got a high-level overview of the SMPL model and used it to create a random 3D human body. Afterward, we went over the code used to generate it. Next, we looked at how SMPLify can be used to fit a 3D human body shape onto a person in a 2D RGB image. We learned about how this uses the SMPL model in the background. Moreover, we fit human body shapes to two images in the LSP dataset and understood the code we used to do this. With this, we got a high-level overview of modeling the human body in 3D.

In the next chapter, we will explore the SynSin model, which is typically used for 3D reconstruction. The goal of the next chapter is to understand how to reconstruct an image from a different view, given just a single image.

9

Performing End-to-End View Synthesis with SynSin

This chapter is dedicated to the latest state-of-the-art view synthesis model called SynSin. View synthesis is one of the main directions in 3D deep learning, which can be used in multiple different domains such as AR, VR, gaming, and more. The goal is to create a model for the given image as an input to reconstruct a new image from another view.

In this chapter, first, we will explore view synthesis and the existing approaches to solving this problem. We will discuss all advantages and disadvantages of these techniques.

Second, we are going to dive deeper into the architecture of the SynSin model. This is an end-to-end model that consists of three main modules. We will discuss each of them and understand how these modules help to solve view synthesis without any 3D data.

After understanding the whole structure of the model, we will move on to hands-on practice, where we will set up and work with the model to better understand the whole view synthesis process. We will train and test the model, and also use pre-trained models for inference.

In this chapter, we're going to cover the following main topics:

- Overview of view synthesis
- SynSin network architecture
- Hands-on model training and testing

Technical requirements

To run the example code snippets in this book, ideally, readers need to have a computer with a GPU. However, running the code snippets with only CPUs is not impossible.

The recommended computer configuration includes the following:

- A GPU, for example, the Nvidia GTX series or the RTX series with at least 8 GB of memory
- Python 3
- The PyTorch and PyTorch3D libraries

The code snippets for this chapter can be found at `https:github.com/PacktPublishing/3D-Deep-Learning-with-Python`.

Overview of view synthesis

One of the most popular research directions in 3D computer vision is view synthesis. Given the data and the viewpoint, the idea of this research direction is to generate a new image that renders the object from another viewpoint.

View synthesis comes with two challenges. The model should understand the 3D structure and semantic information of the image. By 3D structure, we mean that when changing the viewpoint, we get closer to some objects and far away from others. A good model should handle this by rendering images where some objects are bigger and some are smaller to view - change. By semantic information, we mean that the model should differentiate the objects and should understand what objects are presented in the image. This is important because some objects can be partially included in the image; therefore, during the reconstruction, the model should understand the semantics of the object to know how to reconstruct the continuation of that object. For example, given an image of a car on one side where we only see two wheels, we know that there are two more wheels on the other side of the car. The model must contain these semantics during reconstruction:

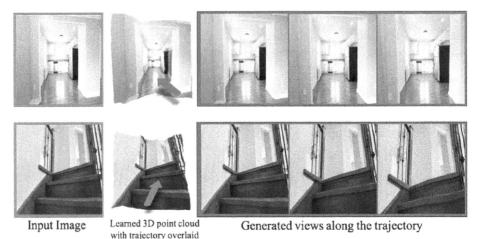

Input Image   Learned 3D point cloud   Generated views along the trajectory
               with trajectory overlaid

Figure 9.1: The red-framed photographs show the original image, and the blue-framed photographs show the newly generated images; this is an example of view synthesis using the SynSin methodology

Many challenges need to be addressed. For the models, it's hard to understand the 3D scene from an image. There are several methods for view synthesis:

- **View synthesis from multiple images**: Deep neural networks can be used to learn the depth of multiple images, and then reconstruct new images from another view. However, as mentioned earlier, this implies that we have multiple images from slightly different views, and sometimes, it's hard to obtain such data.

- **View synthesis using ground-truth depth**: This involves a group of techniques where a ground-truth mask is used beside the image, which represents the depth of the image and semantics. Although in some cases, these types of models can achieve good results, it's hard and expensive to gather data on a large scale, especially when it comes to outdoor scenes. Also, it's expensive and time-consuming to annotate such data on a large scale, too.

- **View synthesis from a single image**: This is a more realistic setting when we have only one image and we aim to reconstruct an image from the new view. It's harder to get more accurate results by only using one image. SynSin belongs to a group of methods that can achieve a state-of-the-art view synthesis.

So, we have covered a brief overview of view synthesis. Now, we will explore SynSin, dive into the network architecture, and examine the model training and testing processes.

SynSin network architecture

The idea of SynSin is to solve the view synthesis problem with an end-to-end model using only one image at test time. This is a model that doesn't need 3D data annotations and acheives very good accuracy compared to its baseline:

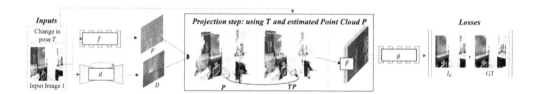

Figure 9.2: The structure of the end-to-end SynSin method

The model is trained end-to-end, and it consists of three different modules:

- Spatial feature and depth networks
- Neural point cloud renderer
- Refinement module and discriminator

Let's dive deeper into each one to better understand the architecture.

Spatial feature and depth networks

If we zoom into the first part of *Figure 9.2*, we can see two different networks that are fed by the same image. These are the spatial feature network (**f**) and the depth network (**d**) (*Figure 9.3*):

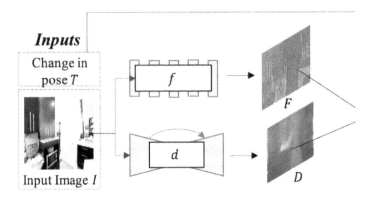

Figure 9.3: Input and outputs of the spatial feature and depth networks

Given a reference image and the desired change in pose (**T**), we wish to generate an image as if that change in the pose were applied to the reference image. For the first part, we only use a reference image and feed it to two networks. A spatial feature network aims to learn feature maps, which are higher-resolution representations of the image. This part of the model is responsible for learning semantic information about the image. This model consists of eight ResNet blocks and outputs 64-dimensional feature maps for each pixel of the image. The output has the same resolution as the original image.

Next, the depth network aims to learn the 3D structure of the image. It won't be an accurate 3D structure, as we don't use exact 3D annotations. However, the model will further improve it. UNet with eight downsampling and upsampling layers are used for this network, followed by the sigmoid layer. Again, the output has the same resolution as the original image.

As you might have noticed, both models keep a high resolution for the output channels. This will further help to reconstruct more accurate and higher-quality images.

Neural point cloud renderer

The next step is to create a 3D point cloud that can then be used with a view transform point to render a new image from the new viewpoint. For that, we use the combined output of the spatial feature and depth networks.

The next step should be rendering the image from another point. In most scenarios, a naïve renderer would be used. This projects 3D points to one pixel or a small region in the new view. A naïve renderer uses a z-buffer, which keeps all the distances from the point to the camera. The problem with the naïve renderer is that it's not differentiable, which means we can't use gradients to update our depth and spatial feature networks. Moreover, we want to render features instead of RGB images. This means the naïve renderer won't work for this technique:

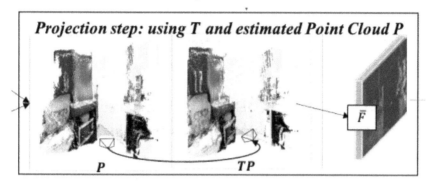

Figure 9.4: Pose transformation in the neural point cloud renderer

Why not just differentiate naïve renderers? Here, we face two problems:

- **Small neighborhoods**: As mentioned earlier, each point only appears on one or a few pixels of the rendered image. Therefore, there are only a few gradients for each point. This is a drawback of local gradients, which degrades the performance of the network relying on gradient updates.

- **The hard z-buffer**: The z-buffer only keeps the nearest point for rendering the image. If new points appear closer, suddenly the output will change drastically.

To overcome the issues presented here, the model tries to soften the hard decision. This technique is called a **neural point cloud renderer**. To do that, the renderer, instead of assigning a pixel for a point, splats with varying influence. This solves a small neighborhood problem. For the hard z-buffer issue, we then accumulate the effect of the nearest points, not just the nearest point:

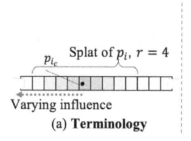

(a) **Terminology**

Figure 9.5: Projecting the point with the splatting technique

A 3D point is projected and splatted with radius **r** (*Figure 9.5*). Then, the influence of the 3D point on that pixel is measured by the Euclidean distance between the center of the splatted point to that point:

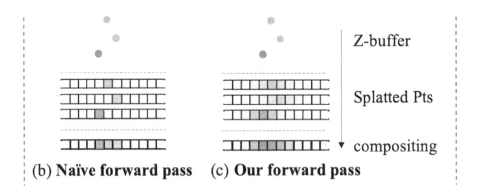

Figure 9.6: The effect of forward and backward propagation with a neural point cloud renderer on an example of naïve (b) and SynSin (c) rendering

As you can see in the preceding figure, each point is splatted, which helps us to not lose too much information and helps in solving tricky problems.

The advantage of this approach is that it allows you to gather more gradients for one 3D point, which improves the network learning process for both spatial features and depth networks:

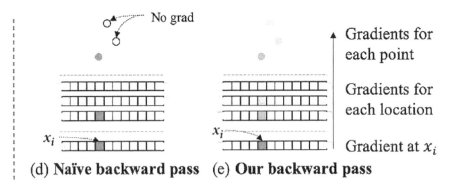

Figure 9.7: Backpropagation for the naïve renderer and the neural point cloud renderer

Lastly, we need to gather and accumulate points in the z-buffer. First, we sort points according to their distance from the new camera, and then K-nearest neighbors with alpha compositing are used to accumulate points:

Learned 3D point cloud
with trajectory overlaid

Figure 9.8: 3D point cloud output

As you can see in *Figure 9.8*, the 3D point cloud outputs an unrefined new view. The output should then become the input of the refiner module.

Refinement module and discriminator

Last but not least, the model consists of a refinement module. This module has two missions: first to improve the accuracy of the projected feature and, second, to fill the nonvisible part of the image from the new view. It should output semantically meaningful and geometrically accurate images. For example, if only one part of the table is visible in the image and in the new view, the image should contain a larger part of it, this module should understand semantically that this is a table, and during the reconstruction, it should keep the lines of the new part geometrically correct (for instance, the straight lines should remain straight). The model learns these properties from a dataset of real-world images:

Learned 3D point cloud
with trajectory overlaid

Figure 9.9: The refinement module

The refinement module (**g**) gets inputs from the neural point cloud renderer and then outputs the final reconstructed image. Then, it is used in loss objectives to improve the training process.

This task is solved with generative models. ResNet with eight blocks is used, and to keep the resolution of the image good, downsampling and upsampling blocks were used, too. We use GAN with two multilayer discriminators and feature matching loss on the discriminator.

The final loss of the model consists of the L1 loss, content loss, and discriminator loss between the generated and target images:

$$\mathcal{L} = \lambda_{GAN}\mathcal{L}_{GAN} + \lambda_{l1}\mathcal{L}_{l1} + \lambda_c\mathcal{L}_c$$

The loss function is then used for model optimization as usual.

This is how SynSin combines various modules to create an end-to-end process of synthesizing views from just one image. Next, we will explore the practical implementation of the model.

Hands-on model training and testing

Facebook Research released the GitHub repository of the SynSin model, which allows us to train the model and use an already pre-trained model for inference. In this section, we will discuss both the training process and inference with pre-trained models:

1. But first, we need to set up the model. We need to clone the GitHub repository, create an environment, and install all the requirements:

```
git clone https://github.com/facebookresearch/synsin.git
cd synsin/
conda create --name synsin_env --file requirements.txt
conda activate synsin_env
```

If requirements can't be installed with the preceding command, it's always possible to install them manually. For manual installation, follow the synsin/INSTALL.md file instructions.

2. The model was trained on three different datasets:

   I.   RealEstate10K

   II.   MP3D

   III. KITTI

   For the training, data can be downloaded from the dataset websites. For this book, we are going to use the KITTI dataset; however, feel free to try other datasets, too.

   Instructions on how to download the KITTI dataset can be found in the SynSin repository at https://github.com/facebookresearch/synsin/blob/main/KITTI.md.

   First, we need to download the dataset from the website and store the files in ${KITTI_HOME}/dataset_kitti, where KITTI_HOME is the path where the dataset will be located.

3. Next, we need to update the ./options/options.py file, where we need to add the path to the KITTI dataset on our local machine:

```
elif opt.dataset == 'kitti':
    opt.min_z = 1.0
    opt.max_z = 50.0
    opt.train_data_path = (
        './DATA/dataset_kitti/'
    )
    from data.kitti import KITTIDataLoader
    return KITTIDataLoader
```

If you are going to use another dataset, you should find the DataLoader for other datasets and add the path to that dataset.

4. Before training, we have to download pre-trained models by running the following command:

```
bash ./download_models.sh
```

If we open and look inside the file, we can see that it includes all the pre-trained models for all three datasets. Therefore, when running the command, it will create three different folders per dataset and download all the pre-trained models for that dataset. We can use them both for training and inference. If you don't want them all downloaded, you can always download them manually by just running the following:

```
wget https://dl.fbaipublicfiles.com/synsin/checkpoints/
realestate/synsin.pth
```

This command will run the SynSin pre-trained model for the real estate dataset. For more information about pre-trained models, the readme.txt file can be downloaded as follows:

```
wget https://dl.fbaipublicfiles.com/synsin/checkpoints/
readme.txt
```

5. For training, you need to run the train.py file. You can run it from the shell using ./ train.sh. If we open the train.sh file, we can find commands for the three different datasets. The default example for KITTI is as follows:

```
python train.py --batch-size 32 \
        --folder 'temp' --num_workers 4  \
        --resume --dataset 'kitti' --use_inv_z \
        --use_inverse_depth \
        --accumulation 'alphacomposite' \
        --model_type 'zbuffer_pts' \
        --refine_model_type 'resnet_256W8UpDown64'  \
        --norm_G 'sync:spectral_batch' \
        --gpu_ids 0,1 --render_ids 1 \
        --suffix '' --normalize_image --lr 0.0001
```

You can play with parameters and datasets and try to simulate the results of the original model. When the training process is complete, you can use your new model for evaluation.

6. For the evaluation, first, we need to have generated ground-truth images. To get that, we need to run the following code:

```
export KITTI=${KITTI_HOME}/dataset_kitti/images
python evaluation/eval_kitti.py --old_model ${OLD_MODEL}
--result_folder ${TEST_FOLDER}
```

We need to set the path where the results will be saved instead of TEST_FOLDER.

The first line exports a new variable, named KITTI, with the path of the images to the dataset. The next script creates the generated and ground-truth pairs for each image:

Losses

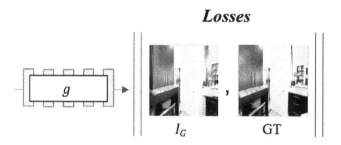

I_G GT

Figure 9.10: An example of the output of eval_kitti.py

The first image is the input image, and the second image is the ground truth. The third image is the network output. As you might have noticed, the camera was moved forward slightly, and for this specific case, the model output seems very well generated.

7. However, we need some numerical representation to understand how well the network works. That is why we need to run the evaluation/evaluate_perceptualsim.py file, which will calculate the accuracy:

```
python evaluation/evaluate_perceptualsim.py \
      --folder ${TEST_FOLDER} \
      --pred_image im_B.png \
      --target_image im_res.png \
      --output_file kitti_results
```

The preceding command will help to evaluate the model given the path to test images, where one of them is the predicted image and the other one is the target image.

The output from my test is as follows:

```
Perceptual similarity for ./DATA/dataset_kitti/test_
folder/:  2.0548
PSNR for /DATA/dataset_kitti/test_folder/:  16.7344
SSIM for /DATA/dataset_kitti/test_folder/:  0.5232
```

One of the metrics used in the evaluation is perceptual similarity, which measures distance in the VGG feature space. The closer to zero, the higher the similarity between images. PSNR is the next metric to measure image reconstruction. It calculates the ratio between the maximum signal power and the power of distorting noise, which, in our case, is the reconstructed image. Finally, the **Structural Similarity Index** (**SSIM**) is a metric that quantifies the deterioration in image quality.

8. Next, we can use a pre-trained model for inference. We need an input image that we will use for inference:

Figure 9.11: The input image for inference

9. Next, we will use the `realestate` model to generate a new image. First, we need to set up the model.

The codes for setting up the model can be found in the GitHub repository in a file called `set_up_model_for_inference.py`.

To set up the model, first, we need to import all the necessary packages:

```
import torch
import torch.nn as nn
import sys
sys.path.insert(0, './synsin')

import os
os.environ['DEBUG'] = '0'

from synsin.models.networks.sync_batchnorm import
convert_model
from synsin.models.base_model import BaseModel
from synsin.options.options import get_model
```

10. Next, we are going to create a function that takes the model path as an input and outputs the model ready for inference. We will break the whole function into smaller chunks to understand the code better. However, the complete function can be found on GitHub:

```
torch.backends.cudnn.enabled = True
opts = torch.load(model_path)['opts']
opts.render_ids = [1]
 torch_devices = [int(gpu_id.strip()) for gpu_id in
opts.gpu_ids.split(",")]
device = 'cuda:' + str(torch_devices[0])
```

Here, we enable the cudnn package and define the device on which the model will be working. Also, the second line imports the model, allowing it to gain access to all the options set for the training, which can be modified if needed. Note that `render_ids` refers to the GPU ID, which, in some cases, might be different for users with different hardware setups.

11. Next, we define the model:

```
model = get_model(opts)
if 'sync' in opts.norm_G:
model = convert_model(model)
model = nn.DataParallel(model,        torch_devices[0:1]).
cuda()
else:
    model = nn.DataParallel(model, torch_devices[0:1]).
cuda()
```

The `get_model` function is imported from the `options.py` file, which loads the weights and returns the final model. Then, from `options`, we check whether we have a synchronized model, which means we are running the model on different machines. If we have it, we run the `convert_model` function, which takes the model and replaces all the `BatchNorm` modules with the `SunchronizedBatchNorm` modules.

12. Finally, we load the model:

```
#  Load the original model to be tested
model_to_test = BaseModel(model, opts)
model_to_test.load_state_dict(torch.load(MODEL_PATH)
['state_dict'])
model_to_test.eval()
print("Loaded model")
```

The `BaseModel` function sets up the final mode. Depending on the train or test mode, it can set the optimizer and initialize the weights. In our case, it will set up the model for test mode.

All this code is summed up in one function called `synsin_model`, which we will import for inference.

The following code is from the `inference_unseen_image.py` file. We will write a function that takes the model path, the test image, and the new view transformation parameters and will output the new image from the new view. If we specify the `save_path` parameter, it will automatically save the output image.

13. Again, we will first import all the modules needed for inference:

```
import matplotlib.pyplot as plt
import quaternion
import torch
import torch.nn as nn
import torchvision.transforms as transforms


from PIL import Image
from set_up_model_for_inference import synsin_model
```

14. Next, we set up the model and create the data transformation for preprocessing:

```
model_to_test = synsin_model(path_to_model)
    # Load the image
    transform = transforms.Compose([
        transforms.Resize((256,256)),
        transforms.ToTensor(),
        transforms.Normalize((0.5, 0.5, 0.5), (0.5, 0.5,
0.5))])

    if isinstance(test_image, str):
        im = Image.open(test_image)
    else:
        im = test_image

    im = transform(im)
```

15. Now we need to specify the view transformation parameters:

```
# Parameters for the transformation
theta = -0.15
```

```
    phi = -0.1
    tx = 0
    ty = 0
    tz = 0.1


RT = torch.eye(4).unsqueeze(0)
# Set up rotation
RT[0,0:3,0:3] = torch.Tensor(quaternion.as_rotation_
matrix(quaternion.from_rotation_vector([phi, theta, 0])))
# Set up translation
RT[0,0:3,3] = torch.Tensor([tx, ty, tz])
```

Here, we need to specify parameters for rotation and translation. Note that theta and phi are responsible for rotation, while tx, ty, and tz are used for translation.

16. Next, we are going to use the uploaded image and new transformation to get output from the network:

```
batch = {
    'images' : [im.unsqueeze(0)],
    'cameras' : [{
        'K' : torch.eye(4).unsqueeze(0),
        'Kinv' : torch.eye(4).unsqueeze(0)
    }]
}


# Generate a new view of the new transformation
with torch.no_grad():
    pred_imgs = model_to_test.model.module.forward_
angle(batch, [RT])
    depth = nn.Sigmoid()(model_to_test.model.module.pts_
regressor(batch['images'][0].cuda()))
```

Here, pred_imgs is the model output that is the new image, and depth is the 3D depth predicted by the model.

17. Finally, we will use the output of the network to visualize the original image, the new predicted image, and the output image:

```
    fig, axis = plt.subplots(1,3, figsize=(10,20))
    axis[0].axis('off')
```

```
      axis[1].axis('off')
      axis[2].axis('off')
      axis[0].imshow(im.permute(1,2,0) * 0.5 + 0.5)
      axis[0].set_title('Input Image')
      axis[1].imshow(pred_imgs[0].squeeze().cpu().
permute(1,2,0).numpy() * 0.5 + 0.5)
      axis[1].set_title('Generated Image')
      axis[2].imshow(depth.squeeze().cpu().clamp(max=0.04))
      axis[2].set_title('Predicted Depth')
```

We use `matplotlib` to visualize the output. Here is the result of the following code:

Figure 9.12: Result of the inference

As we can see, we have a new view, and the model reconstructs the new angle very well. Now we can play with transformation parameters, to generate images from another view.

18. If we slightly change `theta` and `phi`, we get another view transformation. Now we will reconstruct the right part of the image:

```
# Parameters for the transformation
theta = 0.15
phi = 0.1
tx = 0
ty = 0
tz = 0.1
```

The output looks like this:

Figure 9.13: The result of the inference

Changing the transformation parameters all at once or changing them in bigger steps can result in worse accuracy.

19. Now we know how to create an image from the new view. Next, we will write some brief code to sequentially create images and make a small video:

```
from inference_unseen_image import inference
from PIL import Image
import numpy as np
import imageio


def create_gif(model_path, image_path, save_path, theta =
-0.15, phi = -0.1, tx = 0,
                ty = 0, tz = 0.1, num_of_frames = 5):
    im = inference(model_path, test_image=image_path,
theta=theta,
                phi=phi, tx=tx, ty=ty, tz=tz)
    frames = []
```

```
for i in range(num_of_frames):
    im = Image.fromarray((im * 255).astype(np.uint8))
    frames.append(im)
    im = inference(model_path, im, theta=theta,
                phi=phi, tx=tx, ty=ty, tz=tz)


imageio.mimsave(save_path, frames,  duration=1)
```

This chunk of code takes an image as input and, for the given number of frames, generates sequential images. By sequential, we mean that each output of the model becomes the input for the next image generation:

Figure 9.14: Sequential view synthesis

In the preceding figure, there are four consecutive frames. As you can see, it's harder and harder for the model to generate good images when we try bigger steps. This is a good time to start playing with the model's hyperparameters, different camera settings, and step sizes to see how it can improve or reduce the accuracy of the model's output.

Summary

At the beginning of the chapter, we looked at the SynSin model structure, and we gained a deep understanding of the end-to-end process of the model. As mentioned earlier, one interesting approach during the model creation was a differentiable renderer as a part of the training. Also, we saw that the model helps to solve the problem of not having a huge, annotated dataset, or if you don't have multiple images for test time. That is why this is a state-of-the-art model, which would be easier to use in real-life scenarios. We looked at the pros and cons of the model. Also, we looked at how to initialize the model, train, test, and use new images for inference.

In the next chapter, we will look at the Mesh R-CNN model, which combines two different tasks (object detection and 3D model construction) into one model. We will explore the architecture of the model and test the model performance on a random image.

10
Mesh R-CNN

This chapter is dedicated to a state-of-the-art model called Mesh R-CNN, which aims to combine two different but important tasks into one end-to-end model. It is a combination of the well-known image segmentation model Mask R-CNN and a new 3D structure prediction model. These two tasks were researched a lot separately.

Mask R-CNN is an object detection and instance segmentation algorithm that got the highest precision scores in benchmark datasets. It belongs to the R-CNN family and is a two-stage end-to-end object detection model.

Mesh R-CNN goes beyond the 2D object detection problem and outputs a 3D mesh of detected objects as well. If we think of the world, people see in 3D, which means the objects are 3D. So, why not have a detection model that outputs objects in 3D as well?

In this chapter, we are going to understand how Mesh R-CNN works. Moreover, we will dive deeper into understanding different elements and techniques used in models such as voxels, meshes, graph convolutional networks, and Cubify operators.

Next, we will explore the GitHub repository provided by the authors of the Mesh R-CNN paper. We will try the demo on our image and visualize the results of the prediction.

Finally, we will discuss how we can reproduce the training and testing of Mesh R-CNN and understand the benchmark of the model accuracy.

In this chapter, we're going to cover the following main topics:

- Understanding mesh and voxel structures
- Understanding the structure of the model
- Understanding what a graph convolution is
- Trying the demo of Mesh R-CNN
- Understanding the training and testing process of the model

Technical requirements

To run the example code snippets in this book, ideally, you need to have a computer with a GPU. However, running the code snippets with only CPUs is not impossible.

The following are the recommended computer configurations:

- A GPU from, for example, the NVIDIA GTX series or RTX series with at least 8 GB of memory
- Python 3
- The PyTorch library and PyTorch3D libraries
- Detectron2
- The Mesh R-CNN repository, which can be found at `https://github.com/facebookresearch/meshrcnn`

The code snippets for this chapter can be found at `https://github.com/PacktPublishing/3D-Deep-Learning-with-Python`.

Overview of meshes and voxels

As mentioned earlier in this book, meshes and voxels are two different 3D data representations. Mesh R-CNN uses both representations to get better quality 3D structure predictions.

A mesh is the surface of a 3D model represented as polygons, where each polygon can be represented as a triangle. Meshes consist of vertices connected by edges. The edge and vertex connection creates faces that have a commonly triangular shape. This representation is good for faster transformations and rendering:

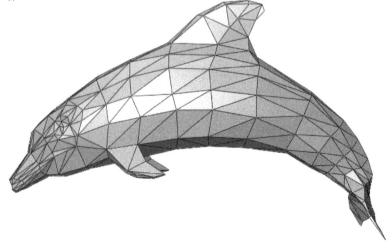

Figure 10.1: Example of a polygon mesh

Voxels are the 3D analogs of 2D pixels. As each image consists of 2D pixels, it is logical to use the same idea to represent 3D data. Each voxel is a cube, and each object is a group of cubes where some of them are the outer visible parts, and some of them are inside the object. It's easier to visualize 3D objects with voxels, but it's not the only use case. In deep learning problems, voxels can be used as input for 3D convolutional neural networks:

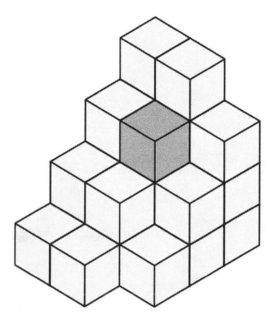

Figure 10.2: Example of a voxel

Mesh R-CNN uses both types of 3D data representations. Experiments have shown that predicting voxels and then converting them into the mesh, and then refining the mesh, helps the network learn better.

Next, we'll look at the Mesh R-CNN architecture to see how the aforementioned 3D representations of data are created from image input.

Mesh R-CNN architecture

3D shape detection has captured the interest of many researchers. Many models have been developed that have gotten good accuracy, but they mostly focused on synthetic benchmarks and isolated objects:

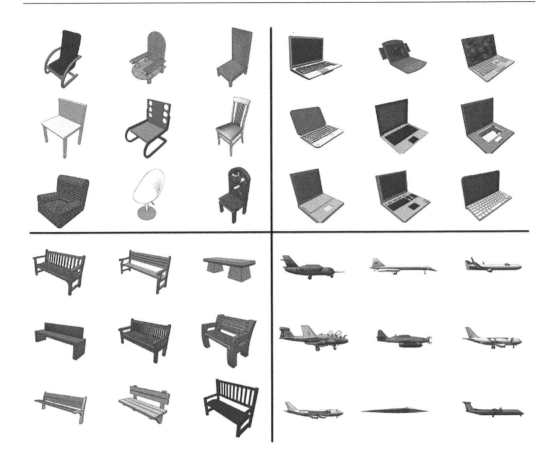

Figure 10.3: 3D object examples of the ShapeNet dataset

At the same time, 2D object detection and image segmentation problems have had rapid advances as well. Many models and architectures solve this problem with high accuracy and speed. There are solutions for localizing objects and detecting the bounding boxes and masks. One of them is called Mask R-CNN, which is a model for object detection and instance segmentation. This model is state-of-the-art and has a lot of real-life applications.

However, we see the world in 3D. The authors of the Mesh R-CNN paper decided to combine these two approaches into a single solution: a model that detects the object on a realistic image and outputs the 3D mesh instead of the mask. The new model takes a state-of-the-art object detection model, which takes an RGB image as input and outputs the class label, segmentation mask, and 3D mesh of the objects. The authors have added a new branch to Mask R-CNN that is responsible for predicting high-resolution triangle meshes:

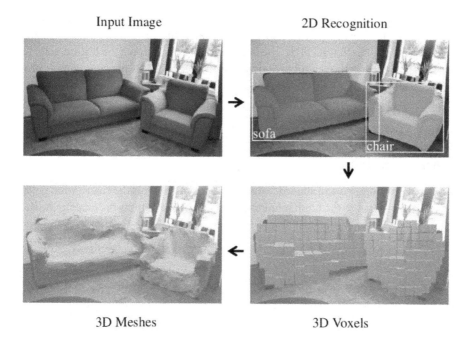

Figure 10.5: Mesh R-CNN general structure

The authors aimed to create one model that is end-to-end trainable. That is why they took the state-of-the-art Mask R-CNN model and added a new branch for mesh prediction. Before diving deeper into the mesh prediction part, let's quickly recap Mask R-CNN:

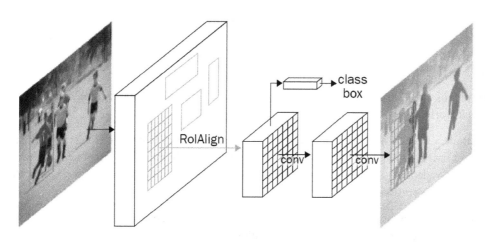

Figure 10.6: Mask R-CNN structure (Reference: https://arxiv.org/abs/1703.06870)

Mask R-CNN takes an RGB image as input and outputs bounding boxes, category labels, and instance segmentation masks. First, the image passes through the backbone network, which is typically based on ResNet – for example, ResNet-50-FPN. The backbone network outputs the feature map, which is the input of the next network: the **region proposal network (RPN)**. This network outputs proposals. The object classification and mask prediction branches then process the proposals and output classes and masks, respectively.

This structure of Mask R-CNN is the same for Mesh R-CNN as well. However, in the end, a mesh predictor was added. A mesh predictor is a new module that consists of two branches: the voxel branch and the mesh refinement branch.

The voxel branch takes proposed and aligned features as input and outputs the coarse voxel predictions. These are then given as input to the mesh refinement branch, which outputs the final mesh. The losses of the voxel branch and mesh refinement branch are added to the box and mask losses and the model is trained end to end:

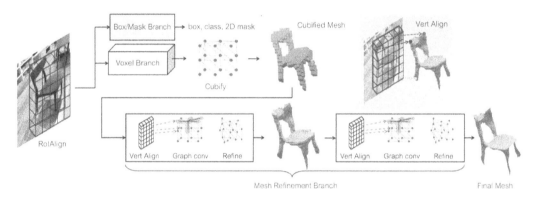

Figure 10.7: Mesh R-CNN architecture

Graph convolutions

Before we look at the structure of the mesh predictor, let's understand what a graph convolution is and how it works.

Early variants of neural networks were adopted for structured Euclidean data. However, in the real world, most data is non-Euclidian and has graph structures. Recently, many variants of neural networks have started to adapt to graph data as well, with one of them being convolutional networks, which are called **graph convolutional networks (GCNs)**.

Meshes have this graph structure, which is why GCNs are applicable in 3D structure prediction problems. The basic operation of a CNN is convolution, which is done using filters. We use the sliding window technique for convolution, and the filters include weights that the model should learn. GCNs use a similar technique for convolution, though the main difference is that the number of nodes can vary, and the nodes are unordered:

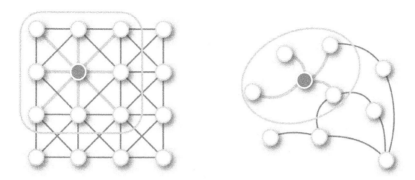

Figure 10.8: Example of a convolution operation in Euclidian and graph
data (Source: https://arxiv.org/pdf/1901.00596.pdf)

Figure 10.9 shows an example of a convolutional layer. The input of the network is the graph and adjacency matrix, which represents the edges between the nodes in forward propagation. The convolution layer encapsulates information for each node by aggregating information from its neighborhood. After that, nonlinear transformation is applied. Later, the output of this network can be used in different tasks, such as classification:

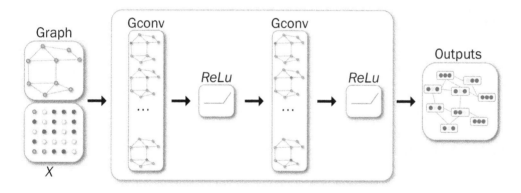

Figure 10.9: Example of a convolutional neural network (Source: https://arxiv.org/pdf/1901.00596.pdf)

Mesh predictor

The mesh predictor module aims to detect the 3D structure of an object. It is the logical continuation of the `RoIAlign` module, and it is responsible for predicting and outputting the final mesh.

As we get 3D meshes from real-life images, we can't use fixed mesh templates with fixed mesh topologies. That is why the mesh predictor consists of two branches. The combination of the voxel branch and mesh refinement branch helps reduce the issue with fixed topologies.

The voxel branch is analogous to the mask branch from Mask R-CNN. It takes aligned features from `ROIAlign` and outputs a G x G x G grid of voxel occupancy probabilities. Next, the Cubify operation is used. It uses a threshold for binarizing voxel occupancy. Each occupied voxel is replaced with a cuboid triangle mesh with 8 vertices, 18 edges, and 12 faces.

The voxel loss is binary cross-entropy, which minimizes the predicted probabilities of voxel occupancy with ground truth occupancies.

The mesh refinement branch is a sequence of three different operations: vertex alignment, graph convolution, and vertex refinement. Vertex alignment is similar to ROI alignment; for each mesh vertex, it yields an image-aligned feature.

Graph convolution takes image-aligned features and propagates information along mesh edges. Vertex refinement updates vertex positions. It aims to update vertex geometry by keeping the topology fixed:

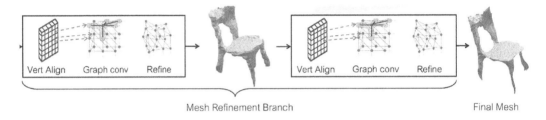

Figure 10.10: Mesh refinement branch

As shown in *Figure 10.10*, we can have multiple stages of refinement. Each stage consists of vertex alignment, graph convolution, and vertex refinement operations. In the end, we get a more accurate 3D mesh.

The final important part of the model is the mesh loss function. For this branch, chamfer and normal losses are used. However, these techniques need sampled points from predicted and ground-truth meshes.

The following mesh sampling method is used: given vertices and faces, the points are uniformly sampled from a probability distribution of the surface of the mesh. The probability of each face is proportional to its area.

Using these sampling techniques, a point cloud from the ground truth, Q, and a point cloud from the prediction, P, are sampled. Next, we calculate Λ_{PQ}, which is the set of pairs (p,q) where q is the nearest neighbor of p in Q.

Chamfer distance is calculated between P and Q:

$$L_{cham}(P,Q) = |P|^{-1} \sum_{(p,q)\in\Lambda_{P,Q}} \|p\text{-}q\|^2 + |Q|^{-1} \sum_{(q,p)\in\Lambda_{Q,P}} \|q\text{-}p\|^2$$

Next, the absolute normal distance is calculated:

$$L_{norm}(P, Q) = -|P|^{-1} \sum_{(p,q)\in\Delta_{P,Q}} |u_p \cdot u_q| - |Q|^{-1} \sum_{(q,p)\in\Delta_{Q,P}} |u_q \cdot u_p|$$

Here, u_p and u_q are the units normal to points p and q, respectively.

However, only these two losses degenerated meshes. This is why, for high-quality mesh production, a shape regularizer was added, which was called edge loss:

$$L_{edge}(V, E) = \frac{1}{|E|} \sum_{(v,v')\in E} \|v - v'\|^2 \text{ where } E \subseteq V \times V$$

The final mesh loss is the weighted average of three presented losses: chamfer loss, normal loss, and edge loss.

In terms of training, two types of experiments were conducted. The first one was to check the mesh predictor branch. Here, the ShapeNet dataset was used, which includes 55 common categories of classes. This is widely used in benchmarking for 3D shape prediction; however, it includes CAD models, which have separate backgrounds. Due to this, the mesh predictor model reached state-of-the-art status. Moreover, it solves issues regarding objects with holes that previous models couldn't detect well:

Figure 10.11: Mesh predictor on the ShapeNet dataset

The third row represents the output of the mesh predictor. We can see that it predicts the 3D shape and that it handles the topology and geometry of objects very well:

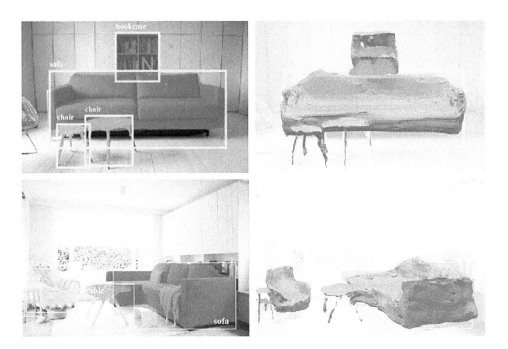

Figure 10.12: The output of the end-to-end Mesh R-CNN model

The next step is to perform experiments on real-life images. For this, the Pix3D dataset was used, which includes 395 unique 3D models placed in 10,069 real-life images. In this case, benchmark results are not available, because the authors were the first to try this technique. However, we can check the output results from the training in *Figure 10.11*.

With that, we have discussed the Mesh R-CNN architecture. Now, we can get hands-on and use Mesh R-CNN to find objects in test images.

Demo of Mesh R-CNN with PyTorch

In this section, we will use the Mesh R-CNN repository to run the demo. We will try the model on our image and render the output `.obj` file to see how the model predicts the 3D shape. Moreover, we will discuss the training process of the model.

Installing Mesh R-CNN is pretty straightforward. You need to install Detectron2 and PyTorch3D first, then build Mesh R-CNN. `Detectron2` is a library from Facebook Research that provides state-of-the-art detection and segmentation models. It includes Mask R-CNN as well, the model on which Mesh R-CNN was built. You can install `detectron2` by running the following command:

```
python -m pip install 'git+https://github.com/facebookresearch/
detectron2.git'
```

If this doesn't work for you, check the website for alternative ways to install it. Next, you need to install PyTorch3D, as described earlier in this book. When both requirements are ready, you just need to build Mesh R-CNN:

```
git clone https://github.com/facebookresearch/meshrcnn.git
cd meshrcnn && pip install -e .
```

Demo

The repository includes a demo.py file, which is used to demonstrate how the end-to-end process of Mesh R-CNN works. The file is located in meshrcnn/demo/demo.py. Let's look at the code to understand how the demo is done. The file includes the VisualizationDemo class, which consists of two main methods: run_on_image and visualize_prediction. The method names speak for themselves: the first takes an image as input and outputs predictions of the model, while the other visualizes the detection of the mask, and then saves the final mesh and the image with predictions and confidence:

```
python demo/demo.py \
--config-file configs/pix3d/meshrcnn_R50_FPN.yaml \
--input /path/to/image \
--output output_demo \
--onlyhighest MODEL.WEIGHTS meshrcnn://meshrcnn_R50.pth
```

For the demo, you just need to run the preceding command from the terminal. The command has the following parameters:

- --config-file takes the path to the config file, which can be found in the configs directory
- --input takes the path to the input image
- --output takes the path to the directory where predictions should be saved
- --onlyhighest, if True, outputs only one mesh and mask that has the highest confidence

Now, let's run and check the output.

For the demo, we will use the image of the apartment that we used in the previous chapter:

Figure 10.13: The input image for the network

We give the path to this image to demo.py. After prediction, we get the mask visualization and mesh of the image. Since we used the --onlyhighest argument, we only got one mask, which is the prediction of the sofa object. This has an 88.7% confidence score. The mask prediction is correct – it covers almost the entire sofa:

Figure 10.14: The output of the demo.py file

Besides the mask, we also got the mesh in the same directory, which is a .obj file. Now, we need to render images from the 3D object.

The following code is from the chapt10/viz_demo_results.py file:

1. First, let's import all the libraries used in the code:

```python
import torch
import numpy as np
import matplotlib.pyplot as plt
from pytorch3d.io import load_obj
from pytorch3d.structures import Meshes
from pytorch3d.renderer import (
    FoVPerspectiveCameras, look_at_view_transform, look_
at_rotation,
    RasterizationSettings, MeshRenderer, MeshRasterizer,
BlendParams,
    SoftSilhouetteShader, HardPhongShader, PointLights,
TexturesVertex,
)
import argparse
```

2. Next, we are going to define arguments to run the code:

```python
parser = argparse.ArgumentParser()
parser.add_argument('--path_to_mesh', default="./demo_
results/0_mesh_sofa_0.887.obj")
parser.add_argument('--save_path', default='./demo_
results/sofa_render.png')
parser.add_argument('--distance', default=1, help =
'distance from camera to the object')
parser.add_argument('--elevation', default=150.0,  help =
'angle of elevation in degrees')
parser.add_argument('--azimuth', default=-10.0, help =
'rotation of the camera')
args = parser.parse_args()
```

We need input for path_to_mesh – that is, the output .obj file of demo.py. We also need to specify the path where the rendered output should be saved, then specify the distance from the camera, elevation angle, and rotation.

3. Next, we must load and initialize the mesh object. First, we must load the `.obj` file with the `load_obj` function from `pytorch3d`. Then, we must make the vertexes white. We will use the `Meshes` structure from `pytorch3d` to create a mesh object:

```
# Load the obj and ignore the textures and materials.
verts, faces_idx, _ = load_obj(args.path_to_mesh)
faces = faces_idx.verts_idx

# Initialize each vertex to be white in color.
verts_rgb = torch.ones_like(verts)[None]   # (1, V, 3)
textures = TexturesVertex(verts_features=verts_rgb.
to(device))

# Create a Meshes object for the sofa. Here we have only
one mesh in the batch.
sofa_mesh = Meshes(
    verts=[verts.to(device)],
    faces=[faces.to(device)],
    textures=textures
)
```

4. The next step is to initialize the perspective camera. Then, we need to set blend parameters that will be used to blend faces. `sigma` controls opacity, whereas `gamma` controls the sharpness of edges:

```
cameras = FoVPerspectiveCameras(device=device)
blend_params = BlendParams(sigma=1e-4, gamma=1e-4)
```

5. Next, we must define settings for rasterization and shading. We will set the output image size to 256*256 and set `faces_per_pixel` to 100, which will blend 100 faces for one pixel. Then, we will use rasterization settings to create a silhouette mesh renderer by composing a rasterizer and a shader:

```
raster_settings = RasterizationSettings(
    image_size=256,
    blur_radius=np.log(1. / 1e-4 - 1.) * blend_params.
sigma,
    faces_per_pixel=100,
)
silhouette_renderer = MeshRenderer(
```

```
        rasterizer=MeshRasterizer(
            cameras=cameras,
            raster_settings=raster_settings
        ),
        shader=SoftSilhouetteShader(blend_params=blend_params)
    )
```

6. We need to create one more `RasterizationSettings` object since we will use the Phong renderer as well. It will only need to blend one face per pixel. Again, the image output will be 256. Then, we need to add a point light in front of the object. Finally, we need to initialize the Phong renderer:

```
raster_settings = RasterizationSettings(
    image_size=256,
    blur_radius=0.0,
    faces_per_pixel=1,
)


lights = PointLights(device=device, location=((2.0, 2.0,
-2.0),))
phong_renderer = MeshRenderer(
    rasterizer=MeshRasterizer(
        cameras=cameras,
        raster_settings=raster_settings
    ),
    shader=HardPhongShader(device=device, cameras=cameras,
lights=lights)
)
```

7. Now, we must create the position of the camera based on spheral angles. We will use the `look_at_view_transform` function and add the `distance`, `elevation`, and `azimuth` parameters that were mentioned previously. Lastly, we must get the rendered output from the silhouette and Phong renderer by giving them the mesh and camera position as input:

```
R, T = look_at_view_transform(distance, elevation,
azimuth, device=device)


# Render the sofa providing the values of R and T.
silhouette = silhouette_renderer(meshes_world=sofa_mesh,
R=R, T=T)
```

```
image_ref = phong_renderer(meshes_world=sofa_mesh, R=R,
T=T)
```

8. The last step is to visualize the results. We will use `matplotlib` to plot both rendered images:

```
plt.figure(figsize=(10, 10))
plt.subplot(1, 2, 1)
plt.imshow(silhouette.squeeze()[..., 3])
plt.grid(False)
plt.subplot(1, 2, 2)
plt.imshow(image_ref.squeeze())
plt.grid(False)
plt.savefig(args.save_path)
```

The output of the preceding code will be a `.png` image that will be saved in the `save_path` folder given in the arguments. For this parameter and the image presented here, the rendered mesh will look like this:

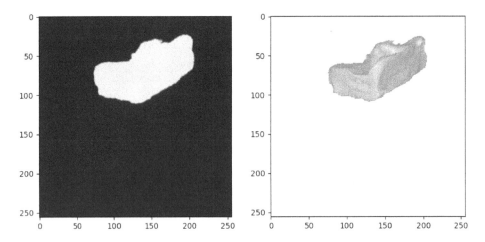

Figure 10.16: Rendered 3D output of the model

As we can see from this angle, the mesh looks very similar to the sofa, not counting some defects on not visible parts. You can play with camera position and lighting to render an image of the object from another point of view.

The repository also provides an opportunity to run and reproduce the experiments described in the Mesh R-CNN paper. It allows you to run both the Pix3D experiment and the ShapeNet experiment.

As mentioned earlier, the Pix3D data includes real-life images of different IKEA furniture. This data was used to evaluate the whole Mesh R-NN from end to end.

To download this data, you need to run the following command:

```
datasets/pix3d/download_pix3d.sh
```

The data contains two splits named S1 and S2 and the repository provides weights for both splits. After downloading the data, you can reproduce the training by running the following command:

```
python tools/train_net.py \
--config-file configs/pix3d/meshrcnn_R50_FPN.yaml \
--eval-only MODEL.WEIGHTS /path/to/checkpoint_file
```

You just need to be careful with the configs. The original model was distributed and trained on 8 GB of GPU. If you don't have that much capacity, it probably won't reach the same accuracy, so you need to tune your hyperparameters for better accuracy.

You can use your trained weights or you can simply run an evaluation on the pre-trained models provided by the authors:

```
python tools/train_net.py \
--config-file configs/pix3d/meshrcnn_R50_FPN.yaml \
--eval-only MODEL.WEIGHTS /path/to/checkpoint_file
```

The preceding command will evaluate the model for the specified checkpoint file. You can find the checkpoints by going to the model's GitHub repository.

Next, if you want to run the experiment on ShapeNet, you need to download the data, which can be done by running the following command:

```
datasets/shapenet/download_shapenet.sh
```

This will download the training, validation, and test sets. The authors have also provided the preprocessing code for the ShapeNet dataset. Preprocessing will reduce the loading time. The following command will output zipped data, which is convenient for training in clusters:

```
python tools/preprocess_shapenet.py \
--shapenet_dir /path/to/ShapeNetCore.v1 \
--shapenet_binvox_dir /path/to/ShapeNetCore.v1.binvox \
--output_dir ./datasets/shapenet/ShapeNetV1processed \
--zip_output
```

Next, to reproduce the experiment, you just need to run the `train_net_shapenet.py` file with corresponding configs. Again, be careful when adjusting the training process to your hardware capacity:

```
python tools/train_net_shapenet.py --num-gpus 8 \
--config-file configs/shapenet/voxmesh_R50.yaml
```

Finally, you can always evaluate your model, or the checkpoints provided by the authors, by running the following command:

```
python tools/train_net_shapenet.py --num-gpus 8 \
--config-file configs/shapenet/voxmesh_R50.yaml
```

You can compare your results with the results provided in the paper. The following chart shows the scale-normalized protocol training results that the authors got:

category	#instances	chamfer	normal	F1(0.1)	F1(0.3)	F1(0.5)
bench	8712	0.120899	0.657536	42.4005	86.0036	95.128
chair	32520	0.183693	0.712362	31.6906	79.8275	92.0139
lamp	11122	0.413965	0.672992	30.5048	70.3449	84.5068
speaker	7752	0.253796	0.730829	24.8335	74.6606	88.237
firearm	11386	0.168323	0.621439	47.2251	85.271	93.8171
table	40796	0.148357	0.75642	42.249	86.2039	94.1623
watercraft	9298	0.224168	0.642812	30.0589	75.5332	89.9764
plane	19416	0.187465	0.684285	39.009	80.998	92.1069
cabinet	7541	0.111294	0.75122	34.8227	86.9346	95.371
car	35981	0.107605	0.647857	29.6397	85.7925	96.2938
monitor	5256	0.218032	0.779365	27.2531	77.2979	90.904
couch	15226	0.144279	0.72302	27.5734	81.684	94.3294
cellphone	5045	0.121504	0.850437	42.9168	88.9888	96.1367
total	210051	0.184875	0.710044	34.629	81.5031	92.5372
per-instance	210051	0.171189	0.70275	34.9372	82.4107	93.1323

Figure 10.17: The results of evaluation on the ShapeNet dataset

The chart includes the category name, number of instances per category, chamfer, normal losses, and the F1 scores.

Summary

In this chapter, we presented a new way of looking at the object detection task. The 3D world requires solutions that work accordingly, and this is one of the first approaches toward that goal. We learned how Mesh R-CNN works by understanding the architecture and the structure of the model. We dove deeper into some interesting operations and techniques that are used in the model, such as graph convolutional networks, Cubify operations, the mesh predictor structure, and more. Finally, we learned how this model can be used in practice to detect objects on the image that the network has never seen before. We evaluated the results by rendering the 3D object.

Throughout this book, we have covered 3D deep learning concepts, from the basics to more advanced solutions. First, we learned about the various 3D data types and structures. Then, we delved into different types of models that solve different types of problems such as mesh detection, view synthesis, and more. In addition, we added PyTorch 3D to our computer vision toolbox. By completing this book, you should be ready to tackle real-world problems related to 3D computer vision and much more.

Index

Symbols

A

B

C

V

W

Other Books You May Enjoy

If you enjoyed this book, you may be interested in these other books by Packt:

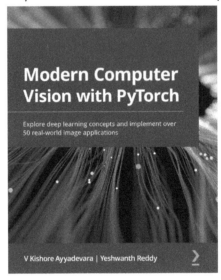

Modern Computer Vision with PyTorch

V Kishore Ayyadevara, Yeshwanth Reddy

ISBN: 978-1-83921-347-2

- Train a NN from scratch with NumPy and PyTorch
- Implement 2D and 3D multi-object detection and segmentation
- Generate digits and DeepFakes with autoencoders and advanced GANs
- Manipulate images using CycleGAN, Pix2PixGAN, StyleGAN2, and SRGAN
- Combine CV with NLP to perform OCR, image captioning, and object detection
- Combine CV with reinforcement learning to build agents that play pong and self-drive a car
- Deploy a deep learning model on the AWS server using FastAPI and Docker
- Implement over 35 NN architectures and common OpenCV utilities

Production-Ready Applied Deep Learning

Tomasz Palczewski, Jaejun (Brandon) Lee, Lenin Mookiah

ISBN: 978-1-80324-366-5

- Understand how to develop a deep learning model using PyTorch and TensorFlow
- Convert a proof-of-concept model into a production-ready application
- Discover how to set up a deep learning pipeline in an efficient way using AWS
- Explore different ways to compress a model for various deployment requirements
- Develop Android and iOS applications that run deep learning on mobile devices
- Monitor a system with a deep learning model in production
- Choose the right system architecture for developing and deploying a model

Packt is searching for authors like you

If you're interested in becoming an author for Packt, please visit `authors.packtpub.com` and apply today. We have worked with thousands of developers and tech professionals, just like you, to help them share their insight with the global tech community. You can make a general application, apply for a specific hot topic that we are recruiting an author for, or submit your own idea.

Share Your Thoughts

Now you've finished *3D Deep Learning with Python*, we'd love to hear your thoughts! Scan the QR code below to go straight to the Amazon review page for this book and share your feedback or leave a review on the site that you purchased it from.

`https://packt.link/r/1-803-24782-7`

Your review is important to us and the tech community and will help us make sure we're delivering excellent quality content.

Download a free PDF copy of this book

Thanks for purchasing this book!

Do you like to read on the go but are unable to carry your print books everywhere?

Is your eBook purchase not compatible with the device of your choice?

Don't worry, now with every Packt book you get a DRM-free PDF version of that book at no cost.

Read anywhere, any place, on any device. Search, copy, and paste code from your favorite technical books directly into your application.

The perks don't stop there, you can get exclusive access to discounts, newsletters, and great free content in your inbox daily

Follow these simple steps to get the benefits:

1. Scan the QR code or visit the link below

https://packt.link/free-ebook/9781803247823

2. Submit your proof of purchase

3. That's it! We'll send your free PDF and other benefits to your email directly

www.ingramcontent.com/pod-product-compliance
Lightning Source LLC
Chambersburg PA
CBHW060547060326
40690CB00017B/3634